Cucina of
Le Marche

❋ A Chef's Treasury
of Recipes from Italy's
Last Culinary Frontier

Cucina of
Le Marche

FABIO TRABOCCHI

WITH PETER KAMINSKY

HarperCollins books may be purchased for educational, business,
or sales promotional use. For information, please write:
Special Markets Department, HarperCollins Publishers,
10 East 53rd Street, New York, NY 10022.

FIRST EDITION

Designed by Jessica Shatan Heslin

Trabocchi family photographs in the introduction courtesy of the author.

Decorative food photographs: half title page (page i) © Photocuisine/Corbis;
pages 13, 33, 55, 89, 127, 145, 177, 209, 219: stock photos.

All other photography by Thomas Schauer

Library of Congress Cataloging-in-Publication Data

Trabocchi, Fabio.

Cucina of Le Marche : a chef's treasury of recipes from Italy's
last culinary frontier / by Fabio Trabocchi, with Peter Kaminsky.

p. cm.

Includes index.

ISBN-10: 0-06-074162-7
ISBN-13: 978-0-06-074162-4

1. Cookery, Italian. 2. Cookery—Italy—Marche. I. Kaminsky, Peter. II. Title.

TX723.T72   2006

641.5945'9495'67—dc22   2006040917

06 07 08 09 10 ❖/RRD 10 9 8 7 6 5 4 3 2 1

In honor of my father, Giuseppe Trabocchi,
and for my children, Luca and Alice

ACKNOWLEDGMENTS

THANKS TO PETER KAMINSKY for his dedication and for his special ability to capture my thoughts about cuisine, my childhood, and my father. Also to Jonathan Hayes, who put me together with the hardest-working agent I have ever met, Lisa Queen. To Thomas Schauer, a brilliant photographer. Of course, to our editor, Daniel Halpern, for believing in the book and gently correcting while encouraging.

To my colleague, Emanuele Fissore, general manager at Maestro, whom I met when he was working as a waiter in London and I was a very young chef. He is part of the heart and soul of Maestro, and I never could have done it without him.

To our wine director, Vincent Feraud, for his brilliant approach to wine, for his advice, for his sense of humor, and his ability to make everyone feel special.

Since the early days in the kitchen, no one has been more dedicated and loyal than sous chef Stefano Frigerio. We have been through a lot together, and I am more grateful than I can put into words. Thanks also to Cliff Dennys, Sean McDonald, and Franck Steigerwald, who have been crucial in constantly improving our cuisine; I will always be proud to have worked with them. A special thank-you to Nicholas Stefanelli, who tested recipes carefully—and often on his own time.

Thanks to Susie Heller for sharing her tremendous knowledge, her skill in recipe writing, and her generosity—in doing more than we hoped to ask. Also to her colleague Amy Vogler. And in New York, to Sophie Menin for getting the recipes in shape in the first place.

Thanks to Judith Sutton for her care and editorial skill. Also, to Ellen Gale, who believed in me since I arrived in this country.

Thanks to all the chefs who continue to inspire me: Michel Richard, Roberto Donna, Cesare Casella, Thomas Keller, Mario Batali, Hubert Keller, Daniel Boulud, and Patrick O'Connell.

CONTENTS

INTRODUCTION

Every chef is a product of a place and a tradition. No matter where your suitcase of knives and pans takes you, these things can always be sensed in your food. They give it soul. ❈ My soul is in Le Marche. ❈ Everybody knows Tuscany, Sicily, and Umbria. Generations of travelers have fallen in love with these provinces. They have built second homes in them, written books about them, and made movies about them—but not about Le Marche. Geography has made us a people apart.

Invariably when I tell people that I am from Le Marche, their next question is, "Where is that?"

As the crow flies, Le Marche is not that far from Rome, a straight shot over the towering Apennines to the Adriatic coast. The catch is, that if the crow didn't feel like soaring over the mountains, it would have to detour north through Umbria and Emilia-Romagna or south through Abruzzo. For a lot of our history, few crows, or people, made the trip. From the most ancient times, however, mariners from Greece and North Africa have found our craggy coast accessible and usually hospitable, and from these seafaring peoples, we assimilated recipes, ingredients, and techniques.

The same geography that set us apart also accounts in part for the rich variety of our food traditions. Rivers divide Le Marche into four natural regions; from north to south, they are Pesaro Urbino, Ancona, Macerata, and Ascoli Piceno. So we are also a people of four distinct regional heritages. Yet as the great food writer Waverly Root observed in *The Food of Italy*, in modern times the variations in the cuisines of Le Marche might be thought of as dialects rather than different culinary languages, because not only does all of Le Marche share a common isolation from the rest of Italy, each province has coastal food, the products of intensively farmed midlands, and the wild harvest of the mountains.

Everywhere in Le Marche, seafood—in dizzying variety—informs the menu. Inland from the coast, in the mountains of the west and north, game abounds. There truffles still grow big and odorous on the roots of favored oaks. And wild boar, who end up in marvelous ragus and sausages, still fatten on the acorns in our ancient forests. Between the mountains and the sea there are gently rolling hills, rich in wheat and farro, peaches and plums, tomatoes, garlic, fennel, basil, lavender, and rosemary. And on the farms, pigs, chickens, turkeys, ducks, and cattle all fatten on the grains and grasses of Le Marche.

It is from those farms, now a vanished way of life, that I inherited my love for food and cooking. You see, my father, Giuseppe, and his father, and every Trabocchi for as long as we have been around, were farmers. They were part of the ancient Marchigiani tradition known as the *mezzadria*. The closest English word would be "sharecropper," but the system meant more than that. It was a communal way of life. And, in much the same way that the rest of Italy, and the larger world, left the Marchigiani to themselves, our landlords and nobles were quite happy to leave the common folks pretty much to themselves as long as they returned a healthy portion of their crops and livestock to the nobility.

In his little village of Santo Stefano, just outside the town of Osimo, where I grew up, my father was known as a great cook. Come harvesttime, when all the neighbors would gather to help each other, he looked forward to cooking up a storm for everyone, as he grilled ducks and quail, porchetta redolent of wild fennel, lamb chops and beefsteaks with the deep flavor that only free-

My father, Giuseppe Trabocchi, with my grandmother Maria Belardinelli

range grass-fed animals have. On special occasions, there would also be fish from the nearby seacoast. Those days were some of his happiest memories.

But all things change, and by the 1960s, the *mezzadria* system could neither compete with the lure of factory jobs in the cities nor stand up to the cut-throat prices of big-time agriculture. My family lost the farm, and my dad became a long-haul truck driver.

Perhaps because we most treasure the things we have lost, his love of that way of life remains with him to this day. Whenever my father was home (usually just a couple of days a week, when his route from the north of Italy down to Abruzzo brought him through Le Marche), he cooked—and I helped. I picked vegetables, and I watered our little garden. Holding my younger sister by the hand, I went to the market,

With my grandmother

where I would say, "My father wants flour and some pork chops," and the kind shopkeeper would load us up. No need for money—my father ran a tab and always paid up.

Pastas, ragus, roast pork, grilled quail, game cooked and smoked in wet hay, nut and honey cakes, delicate sweet rounds of dough fried in olive oil and dusted with sugar . . . my childhood is a memory of tastes and aromas, family and friends, and culinary treasures that could make even a poor kid feel like a rich one at the dinner table.

Today most Marchigiani home cooks are well versed in the food of all of our four regions. But over the centuries of isolation, different traditions and variations on basic themes developed in each of these four distinct provinces. Let me take you on a tour.

Ancona: My Home

THE NATURAL HARBOR OF ANCONA, my home province, lies in the shadow of Mount Conero, which is the major feature of the coast of Le Marche. It is the last upthrust of the Apennines before they plunge into the sea. The name Ancona, like many in Le Marche, comes from Greek—specifically from the word *ankon*, or "elbow", which refers to the Mount Conero peninsula that juts out into the Mediterranean. Because of this accident of geology, Ancona is the only province in Italy where the sun both rises and sets at sea.

Much like Venice to the north, Ancona has always been open to the cosmopolitan influences of the cultures of the eastern Mediterranean and North Africa. For centuries it was part of what the Byzantines called the Pentapolis, or "Five Cities": The other towns were Pesaro, Senigallia, Fano, and Rimini (which today lies just outside the borders of Le Marche). My love for seafood comes from the maritime culture of Ancona, my enthusiasm for the meat and game, fruits and vegetables from the small farms dotting the countryside and, especially, the old family farm in Santo Stefano.

How can I tell you in such a short space what my hometown, the beautiful old city Osimo, means to me? I think some of the feeling comes through in a story that we often told about ourselves. The irony, the self-deprecating humor, the fact that we like to tell such a tale about ourselves reveal more than a little about what kind of people we are.

In the old days, Osimo was the bitter rival of the town of Castelfidardo, situated on a nearby hilltop. As the story goes, during one memorable battle, a squadron of Osimo's eight most dashing lieutenants made a cannon out of a hollowed-out fig tree reinforced with iron bands. They stuffed it with gunpowder and a cannonball and lit the fuse. To no one's surprise, except perhaps the dashing lieutenants, the fig-tree cannon exploded, killing seven of the officers. When the surviving lieutenant was asked by his commander how the assault on Castelfidardo went, he replied, "Well, I can't give you an exact count, all I know for sure is that we lost seven—so can you imagine what we must have done to them?!"

My father when he was in the military

Pesaro Urbino: A Heritage of Art

IF NO ONE IN PESARO URBINO, the northernmost province of Le Marche, had ever cooked a meal, this region would still be a cultural treasure, for it is the birthplace of Raphael. Here, too, one can see the mystical and entrancing paintings of Piero della Francesca. Much of this heritage dates to the ambition of a powerful duke, Federigo di Montefeltro. He was one of the driving forces behind the rebirth of art and culture with which the Italian city-states relit the lamp of learning in the Renaissance.

Federigo's magnificent Ducal Palace in Urbino is considered by any Marchigiano—and many others—as the most beautiful palace on earth. When I first saw it as a young boy, I thought it was one of the wonders of the world.

Federigo was also known for his love of food. But, as legend goes, he was a very suspicious man. He was sure that, given the chance, one of his many enemies would try to knock him off with a drop of poison. To escape this fate, the duke reasoned, if the food were not seasoned before it was placed in front of him, surely he would be able to detect any poison. Fair enough, but as a Marchigiano, eating unseasoned food would be a culinary death sentence. So Federigo, who was also a bit of a cook, made up his own secret seasoning sauce. Five hundred years later, an enterprising gourmand claimed to have rediscovered the ancient formula and made a nice bit of change bottling and selling a honey-based condiment with the Duke's picture on it. True or not, the point is that even our nobility knew something about cooking.

Another illustrious Marchigiani gourmet, the composer Gioacchino Rossini, was also from Urbino. (Tournedos Rossini were named after him—but that came after he had emigrated to Paris.) "I have cried only two times in my life," Rossini is reported to have said. "The first time when I heard Paganini play his violin, and the second on a boat when a truffle-stuffed turkey fell overboard in front of me."

The descendants of the truffles that brought Rossini to tears can still be found in the forest groves of Pesaro Urbino. The boar and venison of its mountains, the fattened hogs of its hillsides, the grand variety of its seafood all contribute to its rich and varied cuisine. It is, again, such variety that typifies all of Le Marche. Today we tend to take it for granted that products can be imported from anywhere in any season. But before modern transportation made this possible, such culinary variety was only possible in areas such as the provinces of Le Marche, where mountain, farmland, and sea were all so close.

Macerata: The Heart of Le Marche

THE PROVINCE OF MACERATA was fairly close to our home in Osimo; its capital city of Macerata was less than an hour's drive away. Perched on a hilltop (as most ancient towns were), it offered an imposing view as we approached in our trusty old car, a light blue Lancia Fulvia. (Even though the car was small, the narrow streets of Macerata made me close my eyes and wince as my father drove through them, always with complete confidence.)

After the Ducal Palazzo of Urbino, Macerata's outdoor theater, known as the Sferisterio (it's no easier to say in Italian than in English), is probably the most famous building in Le Marche. A long oval-shaped edifice, it was originally constructed for the local ballgame known as *pallone al bracciale*. Soon, however, the town fathers realized it was an ideal place to stage every Italian's favorite form of entertainment: opera. The outdoor productions at the Sferisterio have made it second only to Verona's as a summer mecca for opera lovers.

While researching this book, we stopped for a week in Macerata. Every morning we went to a wonderful pastry shop where we drank strong cappuccino and ate fresh croissants. Then, each day, I felt myself drawn to check in with Gilberto, who sold sausages and cheeses about a half block away. He made his own ciaousculo—a marvelous soft pork sausage. He told us that he raised his own pigs, feeding them acorns, which was the way that all pigs were fed in ancient times; the diet makes for beautifully sweet flesh. To prove the truth of his claim, he led us outside his shop to his car and pointed, quite proudly, to the oak leaves and acorns that had lodged below the windshield wipers.

As charming as the city of Macerata is, when I think of the province and its culinary heritage, I see before me the countryside and its wheat fields in the brilliant green of spring. Like its sister provinces, Macerata produces a little bit of everything, but it is famous for, as well as wheat, bountiful olive groves, fragrant honeys, and wild berries. And, winding over the hills and melting into the mist off the Mediterranean, trellised vineyards heavy with tart, fruity Verdicchio grapes. Here, too, you find the unique Vernaccia of the town of Serrapetrona, a red wine in dry and sweet varieties that has long been a Le Marche secret.

One of Le Marche's most famous dishes is our lasagna, vincisgrassi (see page 75). It is mentioned in the work of Antonio Nebbia, whose *Il Cuoco Maceratese*, published in 1784, was the first, and more surprisingly, to date the only comprehensive book on the cuisines of Le Marche.

Just in from the coast, one finds the town of Recanati, which was the home of Giacomo Leopardi, the greatest Italian poet of the nineteenth century. His moods and passions earned him a reputation as "the sublime poet of pessimism." I always found him too sad or, perhaps, bittersweet.

Yet if you think about it, such sadness implies a knowledge of what it is that you are missing. And in that respect, Leopardi was a master at painting word pictures of Marchigiani life when all of Le Marche was still a place of small towns, smaller villages, and countless fields. This excerpt from his canto "The Calm after the Storm" captures, simply and beautifully, that unchanging life.

. . . The storm has gone:
I hear the joyful birds, the hen,
returning to the path,
renews her cackling. See the clear sky
opening from the west, over the mountain:
the landscape clarifies,
the river gleams bright in the valley.
Now every heart is happy, on every side
there's the noise of work
as they return to business.
The craftsman comes to the door,
his work in hand, singing,
to gaze at the humid sky:
a girl runs out to draw water
that's charged with fresh rain:
and, from street to street,
the vegetable seller
raises his cry again
See the sun return, see how it's smiling
down on hills and farms. The servants
open balconies, terraces, lodges:
hear the harness clinking, far off
along the highway: as the traveler's carriage
moves, once more, down the road.

Ascoli Piceno: An Ancient Land

IF LE MARCHE IS THE SECRET ITALY, Ascoli Piceno is the secret Marche. The palm trees and white sandy beaches of its seaport of Grottamare are the beginning of the south of Italy, with its large, flat landholdings and warmer climate. It is an exotic gateway to Sicily, even Africa. At least, that is the way it felt to me once I was old enough to start dreaming of faraway places. When I think of the other provinces of Le Marche, they are in many ways extensions of Tuscany, Umbria, and Emilia-Romagna. The coast of Ascoli Piceno, though, is linked to Abruzzo and pulls me southwards.

The main port, San Benedetto del Tronto, has always had a seafood tradition that is every bit as rich and varied as Ancona's. The rivalry between the two towns centers on whose version of the fish stew known as brodetto (see pages 121 and 124) is more delicious and complex.

Nestled in the uplands, the city of Ascoli Piceno itself is something else again. Here I don't think so much of the south as I think of the old Italy. In Ascoli Piceno, whatever it was that first lured tourists and retirees to Tuscany is still, for the most part, as it has always been. Sit on the sun-drenched main square at lunchtime, enjoying a plate of Ascoli's famous lamb, and you will not see crowds of camera toters and tour groups. Instead, what you see is a wide expanse of honey-colored stone surrounded by medieval and Renaissance buildings and, crossing the piazza, a few people making their way to their afternoon nap. As the coast of this province pulls me south, Ascoli Piceno pulls me back in time.

The Piceni were one of the original ancient people of Italy, back when Romans, Etruscans, and Sabines were all local offshoots of the same nation. As the Romans had the wolf as their guiding spirit, legend has it that the Piceni were watched over by the woodpecker, which was the animal sacred to Mars, god of war—and, today, the symbol of Le Marche.

Ascoli cuisine is as varied as its geography. From the seafood of the coast to the famed Ascolana olives of the midlands to the succulent lamb of the mountain pastures, Ascoli Piceno has been a full partner in the culinary heritage of Le Marche.

In the far west, the province is watched over by the high peaks of the Sibillini Mountains, so named because they were where, according to mythology, the jealous Furies exiled the future-seeing Sibyls. Virgin forests, winter snows, abundant wildlife, berries, and mushrooms preserve some of the landscape and the soul that created a great empire and eternal art works.

Cooking has been my way of continuing the traditions of the four provinces of Le Marche, and the culinary heritage of my farm family. Along the way, I have "gastronomized" Marchigiani cooking a little bit for the increasingly sophisticated palates of well-traveled modern diners. Still, as I moved through apprenticeships with great Italian chefs—some famous and some others who should have been—and then continued into the wider culinary world of Milan, Washington, Marbella, and London, and, finally, to Maestro at The Ritz-Carlton in Tyson's Corner, Virginia, I feel that I have always carried the essence of the Marchigiani way of life in my knives and sauté pans.

Whatever else I may do in life, I am proudest of the fact that I can always say, "I am a chef of Le Marche."

In my first car

Appetizers

and Other

Small Dishes

FRIED STUFFED OLIVES ASCOLANA-STYLE
Olive all'Ascolana

THERE ARE MANY Le Marche dishes that may seem familiar to those who know the cuisines of the other regions of Italy, but these fried stuffed olives are without question an invention of Ascoli. Before any big event in Le Marche, you will find women and girls painstakingly pitting and stuffing the local olives, which are about the size of a large walnut. It is laborious and time-consuming work, but Marchigiani people truly love this dish. And the task makes a fine opportunity for gossip, which is a national pastime in Le Marche.

I find these to be a perfect apéritif with white wine: salty, creamy, and savory. And it may take a lot of effort, or at least a lot of time, to make them, but once you have prepared a batch, breaded stuffed olives can be frozen and kept on hand for parties or big family dinners.

Stuffing

2 slices sandwich bread, crusts removed

3 tablespoons whole milk

10 2/3 tablespoons (5 1/3 ounces) unsalted butter

1/4 pound boneless pork butt (shoulder), coarsely chopped

1/4 pound boneless, skinless chicken, preferably thigh meat, coarsely chopped

1/2 medium onion, coarsely chopped

1/2 celery stalk, coarsely chopped

1/4 pound prosciutto, coarsely chopped

1 tablespoon tomato paste

1 chicken liver, cleaned and cut into small pieces

3/4 cup dry white wine, such as Verdicchio or Pinot Grigio

Kosher salt and freshly ground white pepper

3/4 cup freshly grated Parmigiano-Reggiano

1/2 cup grated mild pecorino

1 large egg

Finely grated zest of 1/2 lemon

1/2 teaspoon freshly grated nutmeg

80 Ascolane or Cerignola olives

4 large eggs

Kosher salt and freshly ground white pepper

2 cups Italian 00 flour or all-purpose flour

2 3/4 cups dried bread crumbs

3 quarts sunflower or peanut oil

FOR THE STUFFING

Combine the bread and milk in a small bowl. Set aside to soak.

Melt the butter in a large sauté pan over medium-high heat. When it begins to foam, add the pork and chicken. Cook, stirring occasionally, for 10 minutes, or until golden brown. Use a slotted spoon to transfer the pork and chicken to a bowl, leaving the fat in the pan.

Return the pan to medium-high heat. Add the onion, celery, and prosciutto and sauté for about 5 minutes, or until the onion and celery are soft and translucent, adjusting the heat as necessary to keep the vegetables from browning. Add the tomato paste and stir for 1 minute. Add the browned meat and chicken liver and cook, stirring, over medium-high heat for 4 minutes. Add the wine and let boil until it has reduced to a glaze. Season to taste with salt and pepper and remove from the heat.

Spoon the meat mixture into a food processor and blend well, stopping occasionally to scrape the sides of the bowl. Squeeze the excess liquid from the soaked bread. Then add the bread, cheese, egg, lemon zest, and nutmeg. Season lightly with salt and pepper and process to a smooth, uniform puree, about 6 minutes.

To check the seasoning, sauté a small patty of the mixture and taste. Reseason the stuffing as necessary. Cover and refrigerate for at least 3 hours, or up to 1 day, to blend the flavors.

FOR THE OLIVES

To pit the olives, slit down one side of each olive to the pit, then carefully cut around the pit to open up the olive like a book. Remove the pit. (Do not use an olive pitter to pit the olives; they would then be too difficult to stuff.)

Using a teaspoon, place a small mound of stuffing in the center of each olive, as if you were replacing the pit with stuffing. Close the olive back up into its original shape.

Continued

Whisk the eggs in a small bowl and season with a pinch each of salt and pepper. Put the flour and bread crumbs in two other small bowls.

Roll a stuffed olive in the flour, then transfer it to the beaten eggs. Using a fork, lift the olive from the eggs, pausing to let it drain over the bowl before placing it in the bread crumbs. Using a teaspoon, roll the olive in the bread crumbs to coat it completely. Shake off any excess crumbs, and transfer the olive to a tray. Repeat with the remaining olives. Cover and refrigerate the olives for at least 30 minutes, or up to 1 day. (The olives can also be frozen. Freeze on the tray until firm, then transfer to an airtight container and freeze for up to 2 weeks. Do not thaw before frying.)

In a deep fryer or a deep heavy pot, heat the oil to 350°F. Line a baking sheet with paper towels.

Use a slotted spoon to add the stuffed olives, in batches, to the hot oil; do not crowd them. Fry for about 4 minutes, or until crisp and golden. Using the spoon, transfer the olives to the prepared baking sheet, and carefully blot off excess oil with paper towels.

Serve immediately.

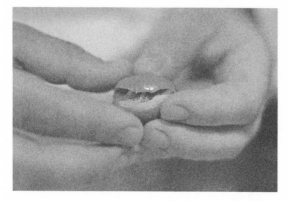 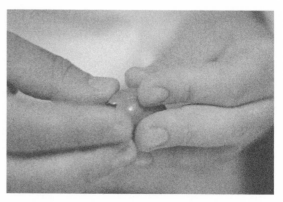

DEEP-FRIED SQUASH BLOSSOMS
Fiori di Zucca Fritti

❀ Serves 6

THE FIRST HOME I remember was in the town of Osimo in the province of Ancona. It was an apartment in a building that was *fuori dalle mura* ("outside the wall"), as Italians say, to indicate a newer neighborhood—meaning from the last five hundred years or so. Buildings outside the wall were not within the perimeter of fortifications that provided protection in the old days. Ours was one of a number of apartment houses that sprang up in the 1960s; when I was quite young, the buildings were less closely packed than they are now, so we were able to grow vegetables on an undeveloped part of the property, giving us the luxury of our own garden in town.

Of course we raised zucchini. Every Italian garden has zucchini, and summer had truly arrived when we could sit on our balcony and, as a special treat, eat the first fried zucchini blossoms of the year.

1¼ cups Italian 00 flour or all-purpose flour	Kosher salt and freshly ground black pepper
1½ teaspoons baking powder	3 quarts sunflower or peanut oil
3 large eggs	12 zucchini blossoms
1¼ cups sparkling water, such as Pellegrino	1 lemon, cut into 6 wedges

Sift the flour and baking powder into a small bowl. Crack the eggs into a large bowl and whisk until well blended. Whisking constantly, add the flour to the eggs in a slow, steady stream, then continue to whisk until the flour is fully absorbed. Whisk in the sparkling water until the batter is smooth and creamy. Season with a pinch each of salt and pepper. Cover and refrigerate for at least 1 hour, or until ready to use.

Continued

In a deep fryer or deep heavy pot, heat the oil to 350°F. Meanwhile, remove the stems from the zucchini blossoms by cutting them off just below the bulb. Starting at the bulb end, slice each blossom lengthwise in half. With your fingers, open up the blossoms to expose more of their surface. Line a plate with paper towels.

One at a time, dip the squash blossoms into the batter, scrape along the rim of the bowl to remove excess batter, and carefully drop into the hot oil. Cook only a few flowers at a time, to avoid crowding. When the blossoms are crisp and golden, about 4 minutes, remove them from the oil using a slotted spoon and place on the paper towels to drain; season immediately with salt and pepper.

Serve the squash blossoms with the lemon wedges so that each guest can squeeze a few drops of lemon juice over them before eating.

CROSTINI WITH TALAMELLO CHEESE AND MORELS
Crostini di Talamello

WHEN I WAS FOURTEEN, I worked for two chefs, Ennio Mencarelli and Silvano Pettinari, who were also my teachers at culinary school. On the weekends in their restaurants, they made me vice president in charge of canapé production for local weddings. It was then that I discovered Ambra di Talamello, a spectacular cheese that is aged in a sealed limestone pit lined with hay and cheesecloth. After a few months, it is unearthed and what started as a white milk product has been transformed into a beautiful golden cheese: hence the name *Ambra*, which is Italian for amber.

1 pound morels (see Sources, page 223)

About 1 cup all-purpose flour (optional)

Six ½-inch-thick slices crusty country bread, such as ciabatta

½ cup extra virgin olive oil

Kosher salt and freshly ground black pepper

1 shallot, minced

1 garlic clove, thinly sliced

½ cup Chicken Stock (page 214)

2 tablespoons finely chopped Italian parsley

½ pound Ambra di Talamello cheese or Italian Fontina, cut into 6 thin slices

If the morels are fairly clean, place them in a large bowl of cold water and gently agitate to loosen the dirt, then gently lift them from the water. Repeat as necessary until the water remains clear, then drain. If the morels seem dry and carry a lot of dirt, toss them very lightly with flour before placing them in the water. Let stand a few minutes, then gently agitate; the flour should pull off the dirt. Carefully lift out the morels and rinse in cold water until the water remains clear; drain. Gently blot any excess moisture from the morels with a kitchen towel. Transfer the morels to a baking

Continued

sheet and set aside in a warm corner of the kitchen to dry for 1 hour.

Preheat the broiler. Using a pastry brush, brush the bread on both sides with olive oil, using 3 to 4 tablespoons of the oil. Place on a baking sheet under the broiler and brown lightly on both sides, turning once. Set aside on the baking sheet. Reduce the oven temperature to 400°F.

Pour the remaining olive oil into a large sauté pan and heat over medium-high heat. Add the morels, season lightly with salt and pepper, and sauté for about 3 minutes, or until they begin to soften. Add the shallot and garlic and sauté for 4 minutes, gently moving the pan back and forth on the burner, until softened. Add the chicken stock, bring to a boil over high heat, and cook for 3 minutes, or until the mushrooms are nicely glazed with the reduced stock. Remove the pan from the heat, add the parsley, and season to taste with additional salt and pepper.

Top each slice of toast with some morels, a spoonful of the glaze, and a slice of cheese. Transfer to the oven and bake for 4 minutes, or until the cheese is melted. Serve immediately.

Fava Bean Salad with Dill, Anchovies, and Capers
Fava Ngreccia

❀ *Serves 6*

IF YOU ARE LUCKY ENOUGH to find them, the small tender fava beans that are available in April and May do not need to be blanched and peeled, as older ones do. Just shuck them from the pod and marinate in the dressing for about 30 minutes before serving.

This is a good salad for a picnic, because it can be made ahead and the flavors will only deepen.

6 oil-packed anchovy fillets	½ cup extra virgin olive oil
1½ tablespoons drained and rinsed capers	Freshly ground black pepper
2 tablespoons finely chopped dill	2¾ cups fresh fava beans (about 5½ pounds in the pod)
1 garlic clove, thinly sliced	2 cups grated mild pecorino (about 8 ounces)
1 tablespoon white wine vinegar	

Bring a large saucepan of salted water to a rolling boil.

Meanwhile, combine the anchovies, capers, dill, and garlic in a medium bowl. Whisk in the vinegar and then the olive oil. Season the vinaigrette to taste with pepper. Set aside.

Prepare a large bowl of ice water. Add the fava beans to the boiling water. Once the water returns to a boil, cook for 3 minutes, or until the beans are tender. Drain the beans and plunge into the ice water to stop the cooking. Drain again and pat dry. Remove the skin from each one by pinching one end and then squeezing out the bean.

Toss the fava beans in the vinaigrette. (The salad can be made up to 1 day ahead to this point and refrigerated. Bring to room temperature before serving.) Spoon the salad into a serving dish, and top with the grated pecorino.

GRILLED EGGPLANT GRAZIELLA-STYLE
Melanzane di Graziella

MY GODMOTHER GRAZIELLA, like my dad, was forced off the farm in the 1960s and moved into Osimo. When she cooked over charcoal there, the way they used to do back in Santo Stefano, the whole neighborhood knew that she was making dinner. The grown-ups would stand around with a beer or a glass of wine, making jokes and grilling sausages, lamb chops, and pig's liver. You could watch the plumes of smoke catch the sunlight and disappear through the trees.

Just before dinner, Graziella would come out of the kitchen with a tray full of chicken or game birds ready for grilling. She would get the ball rolling with some eggplant thrown on the grill. As I write this, I can see myself kicking a soccer ball in the street with my playmates as Graziella took over the grill. This version of her eggplant dish is substantial enough to serve as a vegetarian main course.

NOTE We used to have a trick for regulating the heat in a charcoal fire. Often everyone is eager to eat before the fire has burned down enough. If you keep some ashes from previous fires in a can, you can simply sprinkle them over the hot coals and—presto!—your fire cools down. If you need more heat, shake the grate to loosen the ashes and the coals will heat right up again.

6 large Italian (globe) eggplants	Grated zest of ½ orange
Kosher salt	Grated zest of ½ lemon
1 garlic clove, coarsely chopped	½ cup extra virgin olive oil, plus more for
1 tablespoon chopped dill	brushing eggplant
1 tablespoon chopped oregano	Freshly ground black pepper

Slice each eggplant lengthwise in half. Using a paring knife, score the flesh about ¼ inch deep in a ½-inch criss-cross pattern. Sprinkle lightly with salt and place cut side down in a colander set over a bowl. Cover with a kitchen towel and let stand at room temperature for at least 6 hours to drain.

Prepare a charcoal fire or preheat a gas grill to medium.

Rinse the salt from the eggplant and pat dry. In a small bowl, combine the garlic, dill, oregano, and orange and lemon zests. Whisk in the olive oil. Season the dressing with salt and pepper and transfer to a small serving bowl or sauceboat.

Brush the surface of each eggplant with olive oil. Place cut side down on the grill and grill over medium heat, turning once, for about 6 minutes on each side, or until the cut surface is golden brown and the skin is wrinkled.

Arrange the eggplant on a serving platter and serve warm, each topped with a spoonful of dressing.

NOTE The eggplant can also be grilled in a large cast-iron grill pan on the stovetop.

FLATBREAD WITH CRACKLINGS
Crescia coi Grasselli

❋ *Serves 6*

As FOCACCIA IS TO TUSCANY or Umbria, crescia is to Le Marche. These savory flatbreads can be made with wine, olive oil, and sugar in the dough, and with sausage, potato, or wild greens such as puntarelle, a chicory-like bitter green. Traditionally, because crescia required the cracklings from rendered lard, they were only made in hog-slaughtering season, November to February. Since towns-people no longer kept pigs when I was young, we would buy our crescia from our local butcher. This recipe uses sautéed pancetta as an easy alternative to the crack-lings.

Serve this with cocktails or Champagne, the way you would offer nuts or olives before a meal. It is also great as a late-morning snack for school kids.

NOTE Manteca is soft lard with the appearance of butter. It is often used for fry-ing in regional Marche recipes. It is available in many Latino markets, where it may be labeled *manteca de puerco* (check the label—the word *manteca* is some-times used to mean butter), and some Italian specialty shops.

1¼ cups warm water (105° to 115°F)	2 teaspoons kosher salt
2½ tablespoons active dry yeast	1 teaspoon freshly ground black pepper
5½ ounces pancetta, cut into ¼-inch dice	¼ cup manteca (soft lard; see Sources, page 223)
4 cups Italian 00 flour or all-purpose flour	¼ cup extra virgin olive oil
1½ cups grated mild pecorino (about 6 ounces)	

Pour the water into a small bowl, add the yeast, and stir. Let stand for about 5 minutes, or until the yeast is foamy.

Meanwhile, sauté the pancetta in a nonstick skillet over medium heat until browned and crispy, about 4 minutes. Drain on paper towels.

Sift the flour into the bowl of a standing mixer. Add the pecorino, salt, and pepper. Using the dough hook, mix in the yeast mixture on low speed.

Once it is fully absorbed, add the manteca and knead the dough, still on low speed, for about 10 minutes, or until it pulls away from the sides of the bowl and is smooth and elastic. Add the pancetta (or cracklings) and mix until evenly distributed.

Transfer the dough to a bowl that has been dusted with flour. Cover with a kitchen towel and let rise for about 3 hours at room temperature, until almost doubled in size. (It will not rise as much as a typical bread dough because the lard makes it heavier.)

Generously coat a large baking sheet, approximately 12½ by 17½ inches, with 2 tablespoons of the olive oil.

On a lightly floured work surface, roll out the dough into a large rectangle. Transfer the dough to the oiled baking sheet. Working quickly, press and stretch the dough with your fingertips so it covers the entire surface of the pan. Brush with the remaining 2 tablespoons olive oil. Let rise for about 3 hours in a warm corner of the kitchen, until almost doubled.

Position a rack in the middle of the oven and preheat the oven to 375°F.

Bake the crescia for 15 to 20 minutes, until golden brown. Slice and serve warm.

Flatbread with Prosciutto, Mozzarella, and Arugula
Piadina di Cartoceto

❈ *Makes 8 breads; serves 6*

PIADINA IS ANOTHER Marchigiani flatbread. Cartoceto is a small town on the border of Pesaro Urbino and Emilia-Romagna that makes wonderful piadina. You won't find it further south than Pesaro Urbino, so it was a treat for us when we went with my dad on his truck route. We would stop in the town of Piacenza for lunch and then, before the drive home, we'd get some freshly made piadina at one of the food trucks that served snacks at the side of the road near Pesaro.

As a young cook, I would have piadina as a late-night snack with my best friends Massimiliano ("Red") Bartoli and Gianluca Mazzolani. Red now owns the Williamsburg Diner in Brooklyn, where he serves piadina, and, on the other side of America, Gianluca has piadina on the menu at Barolo restaurant in San Diego, California. I also serve piadina as one of the choices in our bread basket at Maestro.

While this version is my favorite, piadina can be made with a wide array of fillings, including grilled sausage, salami, red peppers, tomatoes, and grilled vegetables.

Dough

½ cup whole milk

4 cups Italian 00 flour or all-purpose flour

1 teaspoon baking powder

½ cup manteca (soft lard; see Sources, page 223)

¾ cup warm water (105° to 115°F)

1 tablespoon kosher salt

Filling

¾ pound thinly sliced prosciutto (about 24 slices), at room temperature

1 pound buffalo mozzarella, thinly sliced, at room temperature

3 cups arugula, tough stems removed

1 to 2 tablespoons extra virgin olive oil

FOR THE DOUGH

In a small saucepan, heat the milk just until warm (about 105°F). Remove from the heat.

Sift the flour and baking powder into the bowl of a standing mixer. Add the manteca, water, and milk, then add the salt. Using the dough hook, mix on low speed for about 10 minutes, or until the dough pulls away from the sides of the bowl. Shape the dough into a smooth ball and place on a plate. Cover with a dampened kitchen towel and let rest in a warm corner of the kitchen for 3 hours.

Divide the dough into 8 pieces. Shape each one into a ball and place the balls on the plate. Cover again with a damp kitchen towel and let rest for 30 minutes.

Preheat the oven to 350°F.

Dust the counter or a pastry board with flour. Using a rolling pin, roll one ball of dough into a thin disk about 10 inches in diameter and ⅛ inch thick. Prick the dough all over with a fork. Place on a piece of parchment paper and repeat with the remaining dough, stacking the disks, separated with parchment paper, as you go.

FOR THE PIADINE

Place a large nonstick frying pan over medium heat. Once it is hot, after about 1 to 2 minutes, place a disk of dough in the pan and cook, turning once, for 3 to 4 minutes on each side, until lightly golden, with some lightly charred spots, but still somewhat soft. Transfer to a plate and cover with a piece of parchment paper or a towel. Continue to cook the piadine, stacking them as you go.

Continued

Place a piadina on the work surface and cover one side of it with a few slices of prosciutto. Top the prosciutto with a layer of one-eighth of the mozzarella. Fold the piadina over the filling to create a half-moon shape and place on a baking sheet. Repeat with the remaining piadine and filling. Bake the piadine for 2 to 3 minutes, or until the mozzarella is warmed through.

Meanwhile, toss the arugula with enough olive oil to lightly coat it.

Remove the piadine from the oven. Open each one and place a small mound of greens over the cheese, then fold over again. Cut each piadina into 4 wedges, and serve warm.

EASTER CHEESE AND BLACK PEPPER CAKE

Pizza al Formaggio di Pasqua

❧ *Serves 12*

BAKED IN A PANETTONE MOLD, this pizza is actually more a savory cake than a pizza, but we call it pizza nonetheless. Traditionally we eat it on Easter with scrambled eggs and shredded mint for breakfast, and then with salami for lunch.

When we were growing up, my dad would send my sister and me to the bakery to choose our own. Actually, there wasn't much choosing involved: Mariella, the baker's wife, knew that Claudia and I always went for the ones with the most cheese. She would make a big show of asking us to make a choice, but she usually kept her hand over the best ones at first. We didn't have a clue that we were being prompted. We'd take our time, inspecting each one carefully, and of course, we'd end up with the ones that Mariella had singled out just for us.

Panettone molds are available in gourmet and specialty bakeware shops as well as online; some markets offer inexpensive but sturdy paper molds (see Sources, page 223).

---

1 ¼ cups plus 2 tablespoons whole milk

¼ cup active dry yeast

½ cup extra virgin olive oil

3 ½ cups Italian 00 flour or all-purpose flour

1 ½ tablespoons kosher salt

1 teaspoon crushed black peppercorns

8 large eggs

1 ⅓ cups diced Caciotta d'Urbino or Italian Fontina or provolone

¾ cup grated mild pecorino

½ cup freshly grated Parmigiano-Reggiano

1 large egg yolk

Continued

Heat 1¼ cups of the milk in a saucepan until it reaches 105°F. Remove the pan from the heat, add the yeast, and let stand until dissolved, about 5 minutes. Add the olive oil and stir well.

Sift the flour into the bowl of a standing mixer. Add the salt and pepper. Using the dough hook, mix on low speed for 2 minutes. Gradually add the milk, mixing until fully absorbed. Add the eggs one at a time, mixing well. Increase the mixer speed to medium and knead the dough for 15 minutes, or until the dough pulls away from the sides of the bowl and forms a soft ball.

Reduce the speed to low, add the cheeses, and mix just until incorporated.

Transfer the dough to a lightly floured bowl and cover it with a dampened towel. Set aside in a warm corner of the kitchen to rise for 3 hours, or until doubled in size.

Butter a panettone mold (or other deep cake pan, such as a 2-quart charlotte mold) and dust with flour. Transfer the dough to the pan, cover with a dampened cloth, and let rise in a warm corner of the kitchen for about 3 hours, until almost doubled; the dough will almost fill the mold.

Place a rack in the middle of the oven and preheat the oven to 375°F.

Combine the egg yolk and the remaining 2 tablespoons milk in a small bowl. Gently brush this egg wash onto the dough.

Bake the cake for 45 minutes, or until the top is golden brown. Let cool in the pan on a rack for 1 hour.

Turn the cake out of the mold onto a serving plate. Serve slightly warm or at room temperature.

The cake can be stored in an airtight container for 2 days.

Soups

PASTA SQUARES IN BROTH
Quadrucci in Brodo

THIS SOUP WAS a traditional quick farmer's lunch, and, as a staple of farm life, it also made its way into the wedding feast, where it would be cooked in the rich stock of the traditional recipe known as *Il Lesso* (page 151). The embellishments for the soup would change with the seasons. In the spring, you would throw in fava beans: in the winter, the bone from a prosciutto. My vote is for this simple yet very satisfying version, with leek, fragrant herbs, and *quadrucci*, "little squares" of pasta. Traditionally scraps of pasta dough, left over from making tagliolini or ravioli, would have been used here. I prefer to make the dough especially for the soup and cut it into small squares.

I recommend a mild young pecorino here, which will not overpower the other flavors as an aged cheese might.

Semolina flour	1 garlic clove, skin left on
Pasta Dough 1 (page 212)	2 shallots, minced
	1 leek, white part only, minced
Soup	2 quarts Chicken Stock (page 214)
1 sprig rosemary	Kosher salt and freshly ground
1 sprig thyme	black pepper
1 sprig sage	1½ cups grated mild pecorino (about
¼ cup extra virgin olive oil, plus more for	6 ounces)
drizzling	

Sprinkle a baking sheet with semolina and set aside. Dust a counter or other work surface lightly with semolina.

Divide the pasta dough into 4 pieces. One at a time, flatten each piece with the palm of your hand and then roll it through a pasta machine, working from the largest setting to the smallest and passing the dough through each setting twice. Lay each sheet of pasta on the semolina-dusted counter and keep covered with a slightly dampened kitchen towel while you work.

Working with one sheet at a time, use a sharp knife or pastry cutter to cut the pasta into ½-inch squares. Spread the quadrucci on the prepared baking sheet, and cover with a dampened kitchen towel. (The pasta can be kept refrigerated for up to a day.)

FOR THE SOUP

Tie the rosemary, thyme, and sage together into a bundle with a piece of kitchen twine. Heat the olive oil in a large saucepan over medium-high heat. Add the herb bundle, then add the garlic, shallots, and leek and sauté for 10 minutes, stirring occasionally.

Add the chicken stock and bring to a boil, then reduce to a simmer. Simmer for 20 minutes.

Increase the heat and bring the soup to a boil; remove the garlic clove. Add the pasta and cook until just tender, 2 to 3 minutes. Season to taste with salt and pepper.

Ladle the soup into warm bowls. Top each with a generous sprinkling of pecorino and a drizzle of olive oil. Serve immediately.

FARRO SOUP WITH PECORINO AND PROSCIUTTO
Minestra all'Antica

❊ *Serves 6*

ITALIANS HAVE BEEN EATING FARRO for thousands of years, and this is a classic Le Marche soup. However, I never knew much about this hearty and delicious grain until I worked in the kitchen of Silvano Pettinari during my student years. He was one of my teachers in culinary school, and he had a restaurant in the town of Corinaldo, a beautiful old walled city.

People from my part of Le Marche often say that the people from Corinaldo are crazy. "It's the winds," is the way the old grandmothers explain things. The following story is typical: A man named Signore Persiano (his name means "shutters") received regular payments from his son in America to build a home in Corinaldo so that the son could one day return there after making his fortune in the New World. Every time the son wrote home, the father assured him that everything was going fine, when in fact all of the son's money was being spent on wine. Finally, though, the son asked to see a picture of his dream house and the father, in desperate straits, had a façade constructed, complete with window boxes and flowers. Standing on a ladder, he leaned out the window and posed for a picture of himself waving happily from the window. He sent the photo off to his son—and the façade still stands to this day.

Choose a young pecorino cheese for this. It will be milder than aged pecorino, as well as easier to chop.

¼ cup plus 2 tablespoons extra virgin olive oil, plus more for drizzling

1 ¼ cups diced (¼-inch) celery

1 cup diced onions

¾ cup diced (¼-inch) prosciutto

1 ¾ cups farro (see Sources, page 223) or barley

2 quarts Chicken Stock (page 214), warmed

Kosher salt and freshly ground black pepper

Six ½-inch-thick slices crusty country bread, such as ciabatta

¾ cup coarsely chopped mild pecorino

3 tablespoons chopped marjoram

In a medium saucepan, heat ¼ cup of the olive oil over medium heat. Add the celery, onions, and prosciutto and cook until the vegetables are soft and translucent. Add the farro and warm chicken stock and quickly bring to a simmer. Cover, reduce the heat to low, and cook for 45 minutes to 1 hour, or until the farro is tender. Remove the soup from the heat and season to taste with salt and pepper.

Meanwhile, brush the bread on both sides with the remaining 2 tablespoons olive oil. Grill or toast (you can use a ridged cast-iron grill pan) until golden brown on both sides.

Place 1 slice of grilled bread in the bottom of each soup bowl. Top the bread with the pecorino and marjoram. Ladle in the hot soup and garnish each bowl with a drizzle of olive oil. Serve immediately.

CHESTNUT SOUP
Zuppa di Castagne

OCTOBER MARKS THE BEGINNING of the chestnut season in Le Marche. The smell of the roasting nuts and woodsmoke in the air is completely seductive. When I was growing up, every town had street vendors who sold handfuls of chestnuts wrapped up in newspaper. For a few pennies, you got to warm your hands and enjoy a piping-hot snack. There are still chestnut vendors in Le Marche today, but far fewer than there once were. You will see them, especially around the holidays, in the town square—*piazza*—on Friday and Saturday nights. We also roasted chestnuts at home in a special pan. There were many cozy nights when we would finish dinner and then hang out around the table, playing cards, nibbling on the warm nuts, and telling the same jokes that we always told—the same sort of often-repeated tales you refer to as "old chestnuts" in English.

Although there are many traditional chestnut soups in Italy, this is my own, one of the first recipes I ever dreamed up. I proudly served it to my family when I was in cooking school in Numana. It is still one of my favorites.

You could, of course, roast and peel your own chestnuts, but it's much easier to buy the vacuum-packed chestnuts available in some gourmet markets and through mail-order sources.

12 tablespoons (6 ounces) unsalted butter	Kosher salt and freshly ground white pepper
2 ounces pancetta, in one piece	½ cup Cognac
⅔ cup chopped shallots	5 cups Chicken Stock (page 214)
⅔ cup chopped peeled celery root	1 bay leaf, preferably fresh
½ pound button mushrooms, trimmed and sliced	1 sprig sage
1 ½ pounds vacuum-packed chestnuts (see Sources, page 223), coarsely chopped	1 sprig thyme
	¾ cup light cream or half-and-half

In a large saucepan, melt 6 tablespoons of the butter over medium heat. Add the pancetta, shallots, and celery root and cook for about 10 minutes, or until the celery root is tender. Remove the pan from the heat and set aside.

Melt the remaining 6 tablespoons butter in a large sauté pan over medium heat. Add the mushrooms and chestnuts and sauté until the chestnuts are golden brown, about 5 minutes. Transfer to the saucepan with the pancetta.

Return the saucepan to medium heat and stir until the pancetta and celery root are hot. Season to taste with salt and pepper. Remove from the heat and add the Cognac. Carefully flame the Cognac by holding a match just above the surface of the liquid. Flambéing the Cognac will evaporate the alcohol; when the flame dies down, return the saucepan to medium heat and add the chicken stock. Tie the bay leaf, sage, and thyme together with kitchen twine and add to the pan. Bring to a gentle simmer and cook for 30 minutes, stirring occasionally.

Remove the pancetta from the soup and discard (it will have given up its flavor to the soup); discard the herb bundle. Working in small batches, transfer the soup to a blender and blend until smooth.

Return the soup to the saucepan, stir in the cream, and gently heat through; do not boil. Season to taste with salt and pepper, and serve.

HEARTY CHICKPEA SOUP
Minestra di Ceci

❄ Serves 6

A RUSTIC AND FILLING one-pot meal, this is one of the soups that sustained poor Marchigiani families for generations. I'd always thought of chickpea soup as a Marchigiani invention, but when I went to visit my wife's family in Spain, I discovered that their national dish, called *cocido*, is based on chickpeas too. It probably has something to do with the Moorish or Arab influence, both in Italy and in Spain. My father-in-law, José Font, makes a rustic version of this soup with lots of tripe. It is quite wonderful. Our version is a little more delicate—and takes about two days less to prepare.

1½ cups dried chickpeas, picked over and rinsed	Kosher salt
1 teaspoon baking soda	¾ cup finely chopped celery
3 tablespoons extra virgin olive oil, plus more for drizzling	¾ cup finely chopped carrots
	2 sprigs rosemary
¾ cup finely chopped onion	1 bay leaf, preferably fresh
1 garlic clove, minced	Freshly ground black pepper
10 ounces prosciutto, cut into ¼-inch dice	2 tablespoons finely chopped Italian parsley
2 whole cloves	⅓ cup freshly grated Parmigiano-Reggiano
2 quarts water	

Place the chickpeas in a large bowl and add the baking soda and enough water to cover them. (The baking soda will help soften the chickpeas.) Soak overnight at room temperature.

Heat the olive oil in a large pot over medium-high heat. Add the onion, garlic, prosciutto, and cloves, reduce the heat to medium, and cook for 5 minutes, or until the onions and garlic are translucent. Add the chickpeas, water, and 1 teaspoon salt and increase the heat. When the water begins to simmer, add the celery, carrots, rosemary, and bay leaf. Partially cover the pot, reduce the heat, and simmer slowly, skimming as necessary, for 1½ hours, or until the chickpeas are tender. Season to taste with salt and pepper.

Ladle the soup into warm bowls. Top with the parsley and grated Parmigiano. Grind black pepper over each bowl, and finish with a drizzle of olive oil.

PASSATELLI IN BROTH
Passatelli all'Urbinate

PASSATELLI ARE SHORT ROUND noodles formed by pressing dough through a potato ricer into simmering chicken stock. In Emilia-Romagna, passatelli are made from a simple dough of bread crumbs, eggs, Parmigiano, lemon zest, and nutmeg. In Urbino, they throw in meat, such as the beef tenderloin here, and some truffles, too. It never ceases to astound me that truffles, which are now expensive delicacies, were once just another everyday ingredient that even poor monks could use to enrich their meals. I'll never forget when I got my first whiff of them (about two seconds before I got my first look at them). I was probably about eight, and we had driven up north to the hill town of Sant'Angelo in Vado. We found the monks from the nearby monastery out in the forest picking truffles, and we went up to one who carried a wicker basket lined with a red-checked cloth that he was using to wrap his treasures. My father reached in and grabbed a big truffle, then held it for me to smell. It was pure heaven. Skip the truffles if they are too much for your pocketbook, because this soup is still very flavorful on its own.

½ pound spinach

2 tablespoons (1 ounce) unsalted butter, softened

Kosher salt and freshly ground black pepper

6 cups Chicken Stock (page 214)

2 ounces beef marrow (optional, but strongly recommended; see Note)

¾ pound beef tenderloin, cut into ½-inch dice

1½ cups freshly grated Parmigiano-Reggiano

¾ cup dried bread crumbs

Finely grated zest of 2 lemons

5 large eggs

¼ teaspoon freshly grated nutmeg

2 ounces black truffles (optional)

Remove and discard any large stems from the spinach. Place the spinach in a large bowl of cold water and move gently to dislodge any sand or dirt, so it falls to the bottom of the bowl. Lift out the spinach. If necessary, repeat with fresh water, then dry in a salad spinner.

Melt 1 tablespoon of the butter in a large saucepan over medium-high heat. Add the spinach, season lightly with salt and pepper, and stir gently until the butter coats the spinach. Cover the pan and cook for 3 to 4 minutes, or until the spinach has wilted. Transfer to a colander and drain, pressing the spinach against the colander with the back of a spoon to eliminate excess water.

If using the marrow, bring enough chicken stock to cover the marrow to a simmer in a small saucepan. Remove the pan from the heat, add the marrow, and cover the pan with plastic wrap. Let the marrow poach for 2 minutes, then transfer to a small plate. Reserve the stock.

In a food processor, combine the beef tenderloin, spinach, marrow (if using), Parmigiano, bread crumbs, the remaining 1 tablespoon butter, the lemon zest, eggs, and nutmeg. Blend until very smooth, up to 4 minutes, scraping the sides of the bowl as needed to ensure even mixing. Transfer to a bowl and season lightly with salt and pepper. To check the seasoning, bring a small saucepan of water to a simmer. Add a small spoonful of the mixture and cook until it rises to the surface. Taste and adjust the seasoning as necessary. Cover the dough and refrigerate for at least 2 hours, or up to 1 day.

Carefully clean the truffles (if using) with a brush, removing any dirt on the surface. Set aside.

Bring the chicken stock (including the marrow poaching liquid, if any) to a boil in a large saucepan. Reduce to a simmer and season to taste with salt and pepper.

Working over the saucepan, press the passatelli mixture through a food mill fitted with the coarse disk, using a knife to cut off 1½-inch lengths of

Continued

dough and letting them drop into the pan. Simmer until the noodles rise to the surface, then remove from the heat.

Ladle the broth and passatelli into warm bowls. Shave the truffle, if you have it, over the soup. Serve immediately.

NOTE To prepare the marrow, soak 8 marrow bones in hot water for about 10 minutes to soften the marrow. Drain, and push the marrow out of each bone. Put the marrow in a small container and add 3 tablespoons white vinegar, a pinch of kosher salt, and enough cold water to cover. Refrigerate overnight, then drain before using.

RICE AND SPINACH SOUP
Minestra di Riso e Spinaci

❀ *Serves 6*

BEFORE I BEGIN MY WEEK in my kitchen at Maestro, I make sure my refrigerator at home is full. I want my kids to have good meals all week even if I am not there to prepare them. No doubt I got this habit of stocking up from my upbringing. When my dad went on the road at the beginning of the week, the fridge was always well stocked. Among other things, you could always count on rice, spinach, prosciutto, chicken stock, and Parmigiano-Reggiano, which were easy to combine in a very simple but filling soup for my sister, Claudia, and me, and I still make a version of that soup today. Back then, I would look at that fridge at the beginning of the week and think that there was enough food there for a month. Now that I am a dad, I understand the psychology: with kids, better too much than too little.

¾ pound spinach

4 tablespoons (2 ounces) unsalted butter

½ medium onion, minced

¼ pound prosciutto, cut into ¼-inch dice

2 quarts Chicken Stock (page 214)

2 ½ cups Carnaroli or Arborio rice

Kosher salt and freshly ground
  black pepper

Extra virgin olive oil for drizzling

1 cup freshly grated
  Parmigiano-Reggiano
  (about 4 ounces)

Remove and discard the large stems from the spinach. Place the spinach in a large bowl of cold water and move gently to dislodge any dirt, which will fall to the bottom of the bowl. Lift out the spinach; if it was very sandy, repeat until the water is clear. Dry in a salad spinner.

Place a large saucepan over medium-high heat and add the butter. When the butter sizzles, add the onion and prosciutto. Sauté for 4 minutes, stirring constantly, until the onion is translucent; be careful not to let the onion brown. Add the chicken stock and bring to a boil. Reduce the heat to

Continued

maintain a rapid simmer, add the rice, and cook for 15 minutes, or until the rice is tender.

Remove the pan from the heat and season to taste with salt and pepper. Stir in the spinach and let stand briefly, until it is wilted.

Ladle the soup into warm bowls. Top each with a drizzle of olive oil and a generous sprinkling of Parmigiano. Serve immediately.

NOTE We use Carnaroli or Arborio rice, risotto rices, because they have the right amount of starch to give the soup a smooth, creamy consistency.

CRAYFISH SOUP WITH GRILLED COUNTRY BREAD

Zuppa di Gamberi di Fiume

❋ *Serves 6*

ONE OF OUR FAVORITE family outings was a trip up to Castelsantangelo, on the Nera River, which was known for its crayfish. We always started early, and perhaps one of the reasons my sister and I enjoyed the trip so much was that we were able to stop in at the pastry shop for warm croissants just as soon as they came out of the oven (at four or five in the morning). Claudia and I would then nap until we woke up somewhere in the beautiful Sibillini mountains with their forests and meadows of wildflowers. In Castelsantangelo, my father would buy a few pounds of crayfish. Then, after the long drive home, we would have this soup.

2 ½ pounds crayfish, fresh (preferably) (see Sources, page 223) or frozen	⅓ cup extra virgin olive oil
8 tablespoons (4 ounces) unsalted butter	1 teaspoon crushed red pepper flakes
3 garlic cloves, thinly sliced, plus 1 whole peeled garlic clove	3 tablespoons chopped Italian parsley
1 teaspoon tomato paste	4 plum tomatoes, peeled, seeded, and cut into ¼-inch dice
5 shallots, minced	Kosher salt and freshly ground black pepper
1 cup Cognac or other brandy	Six ½-inch-thick slices crusty country bread, such as ciabatta
4 cups Fish Stock (page 217)	

If using fresh crayfish, bring a large pot of salted water to a boil. Fill a large bowl with ice water. Add the crayfish to the boiling water and cook for 30 seconds (no longer, or the meat will overcook). Transfer the crayfish to the bowl of ice water to stop the cooking, then drain.

Continued

To peel the crayfish, pull away the tail end to separate the tail from the body: Hold the tail and gently wiggle and pull the end of the tail to release. If done correctly, this will also pull out the internal vein that runs the length of the tail; discard. Peel off the shells, and reserve. Cover and refrigerate the meat.

For the stock, using a large chef's knife or cleaver, roughly chop the crayfish shells. Melt the butter in a large saucepan over medium-high heat. Add the shells and sauté for 10 minutes, stirring occasionally. Add the sliced garlic, tomato paste, and shallots and sauté for 5 minutes, adjusting the heat as necessary to prevent the tomato paste from browning.

Add the Cognac and bring to a simmer, stirring and scraping the bottom of the pan with a wooden spatula or spoon for about 1 minute to loosen any bits clinging to the pan, then simmer for about a minute to evaporate the alcohol. Add the fish stock and bring to a boil. Reduce the heat and simmer for 20 minutes, skimming the surface as necessary to remove any impurities. Strain the stock through a fine-mesh strainer into a bowl, using the back of a ladle or a wooden spoon to press against the shells and extract the maximum amount of flavor from them.

Combine the olive oil, red pepper flakes, and parsley in a large saucepan and heat over medium-high heat for about 4 minutes, until the parsley begins to sizzle. Add the tomatoes and sauté for about 5 minutes, until they begin to soften. Pour the crayfish stock into the saucepan and bring to a simmer. Season to taste with salt and pepper.

Meanwhile, grill or toast the bread. Rub the warm slices on both sides with the whole garlic clove.

Remove the soup from the heat, add the crayfish meat, and let stand briefly just to warm the crayfish without overcooking the meat. Serve with the toasted bread.

NOTE To peel tomatoes, bring a pot of water to a rolling boil. Meanwhile, pre-pare an ice bath. Cut an X into the bottom of each tomato and drop the tomatoes, without crowding, into the boiling water. After 30 seconds remove them with a slotted spoon and immediately plunge them into the ice water. Once they are cool, pull away the skin. To seed the tomatoes, cut each one in half and gently squeeze out the seeds.

CAPPELLETTI IN CAPON BROTH
Cappelletti in Brodo di Cappone

ONE OF MY FIRST chef jobs was in the Byblos Club in Rimini, a resort town in Emilia-Romagna just over the northern border of Le Marche. Cappelletti are tiny ravioli that were made, like all of the pasta at Byblos, by two expert pasta makers, Maria and Elena. Because I showed such an interest in their work, they really took a shine to me. They would stand at the pasta station talking about their kids and trading the juiciest local gossip, and all the while, their hands were a blur of motion as they turned out kilos and kilos of pasta.

After going through all of the preparation required to make this dish from scratch, as we do in Le Marche, you want to make sure that you get all the eating you can out of it. I save the meat of the capon for another meal, to serve with vegetables and Salsa Verde (page 96), or to use for sandwiches or a chicken salad.

Filling

6 slices white sandwich bread, crusts removed

¼ cup whole milk

2 tablespoons extra virgin olive oil

½ pound pancetta, cut into ¼-inch dice

1½ cups diced (¼-inch) button mushrooms

1 sprig rosemary

½ cup dry white wine, such as Verdicchio or Pinot Grigio

¼ pound prosciutto, cut into ¼-inch dice

3 large egg yolks

1 cup freshly grated Parmigiano-Reggiano (about 4 ounces)

¼ teaspoon freshly grated nutmeg

Kosher salt and freshly ground black pepper

Capon Broth

1 small capon (about 6 pounds) or 2 organic stewing chickens (about 3 pounds each)

5 quarts Chicken Stock (page 214)

1 small carrot, peeled

1 celery stalk

1 small onion, skin left on, halved

A handful of Italian parsley stems

2 whole cloves

1½ teaspoons crushed white peppercorns

Cappelletti (makes about 120)	*Freshly grated Parmigiano-Reggiano*
Semolina flour	*for serving*
Pasta Dough 1 (page 212)	
1 large egg, beaten with 2 tablespoons water for egg wash	

FOR THE FILLING

Cut enough of the bread into ¼-inch cubes to give you 1½ cups. Reserve any extra bread for another use. In a small bowl, soak the bread in the milk.

Heat the olive oil in a large sauté pan over medium-high heat. Add the pancetta, mushrooms, and rosemary. Sauté for about 8 minutes, or until the pancetta is golden brown and the mushrooms have softened. Add the wine, increase the heat to medium-high, and bring to a boil. Cook until the liquid has almost completely evaporated.

Discard the rosemary, and transfer the pancetta and mushrooms to a food processor. Squeeze the excess moisture from the soaked bread, then add the bread, prosciutto, yolks, Parmigiano, and nutmeg to the processor and blend until the filling is creamy and uniform in texture. Season with salt and pepper. To check the seasoning, sauté a small patty in a nonstick pan and taste. Reseason the mixture as necessary. Cover and refrigerate for at least 6 hours, to allow the flavors to blend. (The filling can be refrigerated for up to 24 hours.)

FOR THE BROTH

Place the capon in an 8- to 10-quart stockpot. Add the chicken stock and gently bring to a simmer over medium-low heat; skim frequently to remove any impurities that rise to the surface. Add the carrot, celery, onion, parsley, cloves, and peppercorns. Simmer gently, continuing to skim as necessary, for 5 hours. Do not stir, as that would cloud the stock.

Continued

Carefully lift the capon from the stock and reserve for another use (see note on page 50). Strain the broth through a fine-mesh strainer into a small pot or other container. Let cool (to cool the stock quickly, set the pot in a bowl or sink of ice water, stirring occasionally), then cover and refrigerate. (The stock can be refrigerated for 2 to 3 days or frozen for longer storage.)

FOR THE CAPPELLETTI

Sprinkle one or two baking sheets with semolina and set aside. Dust a counter or other work surface lightly with semolina.

Divide the pasta dough into 4 pieces. One at a time, flatten each piece of dough with the palm of your hand and then roll it through a pasta machine, working from the largest setting to the smallest and passing the dough through each setting twice. Lay each sheet of pasta on the semolina-dusted counter and keep covered with a slightly dampened kitchen towel.

Dust a work surface with flour. Lay 1 sheet of pasta on the work surface (keep the remaining sheets covered) and use a 1½-inch round cookie cutter to cut out disks of dough.

Spoon the chilled filling into a pastry bag fitted with a plain ½-inch tip. (If you do not have a pastry bag, use a small spoon.) Pipe 1 teaspoon of filling (the size of a small cherry) in the center of each disk.

Using a pastry brush, lightly brush the exposed surface of each disk with egg wash. Fold each one over to form a half-circle, and press the edges together with your thumb and forefinger to seal. One at a time, lay the cappelletti across your forefinger, then fold the two sides down and around your finger, dab a bit of egg wash on the pasta tips, and press to seal together. The finished pasta will resemble a belly button. Transfer the cappelletti to the prepared baking sheet and cover with a kitchen towel. Repeat with the remaining pasta dough and filling, transferring the cappelletti to the baking sheet(s). If not using immediately, refrigerate, covered, until ready to cook.

TO SERVE

Bring the broth to a boil in a small pot. Add the cappelletti. Once the cappelletti have risen to the surface, cook them for 4 minutes longer. Use a slotted spoon to divide the cappelletti among six warm soup bowls. Ladle the capon broth over the pasta. Top with grated Parmigiano, and serve immediately.

Pasta and Risotto

"BRAISED" PASTA WITH TOMATOES AND RAMPS

Penne al Pomodoro e Aglio Orsino

❋ *Serves 6*

THIS UNUSUAL METHOD of cooking pasta, which is similar to the way the liquid is added when making a risotto, works beautifully with small shapes like penne or orecchiete. A really good imported pasta will be quite porous, which allows it to soak up liquid bit by bit, just as rice does in risotto. But slow-dried artisanal pastas also have enough of a finish that they maintain their shape as they become perfectly al dente. Adding the liquid to the pasta a little at a time as it cooks means some of the starch in the pasta gradually seeps out, making for rich creaminess in the sauce. For this dish to shine, be sure to use a high-quality extra-virgin olive oil, as well as slow-dried pasta from Italy.

This braising technique works with many sauces. I even use it for carbonara (then I fold in the eggs at the end). And in the summer you can make this dish with red ripe tomatoes and lots of basil, omitting the ramps.

6 ramps (or 6 stalks spring garlic)	1 recipe Basic Tomato Sauce (page 210)
3 cups Chicken Stock (page 214)	2 garlic cloves, thinly sliced
Kosher salt	12 plum tomatoes, peeled, seeded, and cut into large chunks, or 12 canned plum tomatoes, halved, seeded, and cut into chunks
1 cup extra virgin olive oil	
1 shallot, minced	
1 pound penne	Freshly ground white pepper
1 cup dry white wine, such as Verdicchio or Pinot Grigio	12 basil leaves, torn into bits

Rinse the ramps (or spring garlic) in cool water and pat dry. Trim the root ends. Separate the stems and leaves, and slice the stems into 3 pieces each. Cut the leaves into pieces roughly the same size as the penne. Place the stems and leaves in a bowl, cover with a damp paper towel, and refrigerate.

Bring the chicken stock to a simmer in a medium saucepan. Season lightly with salt, and keep warm.

Heat ½ cup of the olive oil in a large saucepan over medium-high heat. Add the shallot and sweat until soft and translucent, about 3 minutes. Add the penne and toast for 1 minute, stirring constantly with a wooden spatula or spoon. Add the white wine and bring to a simmer, stirring. Simmer until the wine has almost completely evaporated. Add 1½ cups of the chicken stock and bring to a simmer. Cook, stirring occasionally, for 5 minutes, then add the sauce. Bring back to a simmer, stirring gently from time to time. Slowly add the remaining chicken stock ½ cup at a time, cooking and stirring occasionally as you would with risotto, until the penne is al dente and there is still a little cooking liquid in the pan, about 10 minutes total.

Meanwhile, combine the remaining ½ cup olive oil and the thinly sliced garlic in a large sauté pan and heat over medium-high heat. When the garlic begins to sizzle, add the tomatoes, season with salt and pepper, and sauté for 3 minutes. Add the ramps (or spring garlic) and cook for 1 minute more.

Add the tomatoes and ramps to the penne. Adjust the heat to medium-high and cook for 2 minutes to allow the pasta to absorb some of the sauce. Season to taste with salt and pepper, add the basil, and serve immediately.

TAGLIOLINI WITH WHITE TRUFFLES
Tagliolini al Tartufo Bianco d'Acqualagna

❋ *Serves 6*

YOU CANNOT MAKE a more expensive pasta dish than this, but that is not as important as the fact that you cannot make a more delicious pasta dish. Although I had eaten black truffles when I was a child, I'd never seen a white truffle until I went to work for Silvano Pettinari in Corinaldo. I can still recall the sound of the little truffle slicer as the shavings flew off in beautiful funky-smelling flakes. Eventually, because of my obvious enthusiasm, and because he was a nice guy, Silvano gave me a truffle. I took it home and cooked this dish. My father's comment after what was his first taste of white truffle was, "*Bestiale!*"—hard to translate, but it conveyed the emotion of "Pretty darn great!"

Semolina flour for sprinkling

A double recipe of Pasta Dough 2 (page 213)

2½ ounces white truffles

1¼ cups Chicken Stock (page 214)

12 tablespoons (6 ounces) unsalted butter

Kosher salt

1½ cups freshly grated Parmigiano-Reggiano (about 6 ounces)

Sprinkle a baking sheet with semolina and set aside. Dust a counter or other work surface lightly with semolina.

Divide the pasta dough into 4 pieces. One at a time, flatten each piece of dough under the palm of your hand and then roll it through a pasta machine, working from the largest setting to the smallest and passing the dough through each setting twice. Lay the completed sheets of pasta on the semolina-dusted counter and keep covered with a slightly dampened kitchen towel as you work.

Cut the sheets of dough into 10-inch-long pieces. Using the pasta machine, cut the sheets into ⅛-inch-wide ribbons. Transfer the pasta to the prepared baking sheet. Cover with a dampened towel, and refrigerate until ready to use.

Bring a large pot of salted water to a rolling boil.

Gently clean the white truffles with a brush, removing any dirt on the surface. Set aside to come to room temperature while you prepare the sauce.

Add the chicken stock to a large sauté pan, place over medium-high heat, and bring to a boil. Boil to reduce the liquid by one-third. Reduce the heat to low, add the butter, and gently move the pan back and forth on the burner until the butter melts and is incorporated into the stock. Season to taste with salt and remove from the heat.

Add the tagliolini to the boiling water and immediately stir to prevent the pasta from sticking together. Cook for about 3 minutes, or until the tagliolini begin to rise to the surface, about 3 minutes. Set aside about ½ cup of the cooking water, and drain the pasta in a colander; shake the colander to drain well.

Carefully rewarm the sauce over low heat. (If it gets too hot, the sauce could separate; if that should happen, swirl in some of the reserved pasta water to re-emulsify.) Add the pasta and Parmigiano, and toss well to coat.

Divide the pasta among six warm plates. Use a truffle slicer or a small hand-held mandoline to shave the truffles over the pasta. Serve immediately.

RAVIOLI WITH FRESH HERBS AND GREENS IN LEMON BUTTER

Ravioli di San Leo

❀ Serves 6

IF I ASKED YOU to picture a medieval village, I think something like the little town of San Leo, in the northern part of Le Marche, would come to mind. Rising up from a rocky cliff, it is so inaccessible that it was used for centuries as a prison. In fact Count Cagliostoro, the flamboyant eighteenth-century magician—some say he practiced black magic—was imprisoned here until his death. Since his followers believed he had found the secret of eternal life, his passing created a crisis of faith for his disciples.

San Leo is also the home of these ravioli, made with chard, spinach, and fresh ricotta. They have always been a favorite of my family, particularly because of their use of lots of fresh herbs including the mint-like nepitella, which is popular all over Italy. If you can't find it (which will probably be the case unless you grow it in your own garden), you can substitute mint, which is stronger, but close enough.

This is best made with high-quality fresh ricotta, which you can find in Italian specialty markets and some shops. Also, since ricotta has a high water content, the ravioli are best assembled just before serving.

Filling

½ pound spinach

¼ pound Swiss chard

4 tablespoons (2 ounces) unsalted butter

Kosher salt and freshly ground black pepper

⅓ cup extra virgin olive oil

½ cup fresh ricotta

2 large egg yolks, beaten

1½ cups finely chopped mixed herbs, such as Italian parsley, marjoram, nepitella, mint, tarragon, basil, and/or chives

Semolina flour for dusting

A double recipe of Pasta Dough 1 (page 212)

1 large egg, beaten

Sauce

10⅔ tablespoons (5⅓ ounces) unsalted butter

1 tablespoon grated lemon zest

1 teaspoon ground cinnamon

Kosher salt and freshly ground white pepper

1 cup freshly grated Parmigiano-Reggiano (about 4 ounces)

FOR THE FILLING

Remove the tough stems from the spinach and Swiss chard and discard. Place the leaves in a large bowl of cold water and swish to release any dirt, then lift out the leaves. If the leaves seem very dirty, repeat. Dry in a salad spinner.

Melt 1 tablespoon of the butter in a large saucepan over medium heat. Add one-quarter of the spinach and chard and toss with a fork, lightly coating the leaves with butter. Season to taste with salt and pepper and cover tightly. Let the spinach and chard steam for about 2 minutes, or until wilted. Transfer the greens to a colander and drain well, pressing with the back of a spoon to eliminate excess water. Repeat the process three more times with the remaining spinach and chard, using another tablespoon of butter for each batch. Transfer the greens to a cutting board and coarsely chop.

In a large bowl, combine the olive oil, ricotta, and yolks. Add the greens and chopped herbs and mix well. Cover and refrigerate for at least 2 hours, or until ready to use.

FOR THE RAVIOLI

Sprinkle a baking sheet with semolina and set aside. Dust a counter or other work surface lightly with semolina.

Divide the pasta dough into 4 pieces. One at a time, flatten each piece of dough under the palm of your hand and then roll it through a pasta machine, working from the largest setting to the smallest and passing the dough through each setting twice. Lay the completed sheets of pasta on the semolina-dusted counter and keep covered with a slightly dampened kitchen towel as you work.

Continued

If necessary, trim the sheets of pasta so that they are all the same length. Place 1 sheet of pasta on the semolina-dusted work surface. Working quickly, place heaping teaspoons of filling down the center of the dough, starting 1½ inches from one end of the sheet and spacing them 3 inches apart. Brush the exposed dough around the filling lightly with the beaten egg, then carefully drape a second sheet of dough over the sheet with the filling. Using your fingers, press down around the mounds of filling to force out any air bubbles. Using a pasta cutter or a sharp knife, cut around the mounds of filling to form 3-inch square ravioli. Press the edges between your thumb and forefinger to seal. Transfer the ravioli to the semolina-dusted baking sheet, and repeat with the remaining pasta sheets and filling. Cover with a slightly dampened kitchen towel. If not cooking the ravioli immediately, refrigerate, covered, until ready to proceed.

Bring a large pot of salted water to a boil. Add the ravioli and lower the heat to maintain a gentle boil, so as not to damage the ravioli. Once the ravioli have floated to the surface, cook for about 3 minutes longer, or until the pasta is just cooked.

MEANWHILE, FOR THE SAUCE

Melt the butter in a large sauté pan over medium-low heat. Add the lemon zest and cinnamon. Season to taste with salt and pepper. Keep warm over very low heat.

When the ravioli are cooked, using a slotted spoon, transfer them to a colander and drain well. Gently fold the ravioli and Parmigiano into the sauce.

Serve the ravioli on a platter or in individual bowls.

Spaghetti with Mussels
Spaghetti con i Moscioli

❋ *Serves 6*

IN MY TEENS I worked at a beach club, and this was one of the pastas we had on the menu. (I had a rather varied "career" at the club: In the morning I set up the beach umbrellas; in the afternoon I cleaned kilos of mussels; in the evening I made all the dough for the pizzas the club served—and, in between, I waited tables.) The tomato-based pasta sauces all looked the same, so when I helped my boss, Sandro Pierini, serve them, I never went by the name—I went by the smell. One night there were several plates of pasta orders that I was told to deliver to one of the tables. I took one sniff and said, "I think that's not right. This is *arrabbiata*, and it goes to table sixteen." Sandro's wife, Giada, looked up and said to him, "This kid is going to be good someday, you know." I didn't give it much thought at the time, but now that I'm a chef, Giada's words have come to mean a lot to me.

You will never see the word *moscioli* for mussels on any Italian menu outside of Le Marche. Instead, it will be *cozze*. *Moscioli* is another of the words in the Marchigiani dialect developed during the centuries of semi-isolation.

---

1 pound spaghettini

3¼ pounds mussels, scrubbed and debearded

2½ cups dry white wine, such as Verdicchio or Pinot Grigio

3 garlic cloves, sliced paper-thin

¾ cup extra virgin olive oil

3 large ripe tomatoes, peeled, seeded, and diced

3 tablespoons finely chopped Italian parsley

Place a large heavy pot over high heat. The mussels should be cooked in a single layer: If necessary use two pots, or cook the mussels (in the wine) in batches. When the pot is extremely hot, carefully add the mussels and the wine. Cover tightly, and cook just until the mussels open. Remove from the heat, and pour the mussels into a colander set over a bowl to catch the liquid. Set the mussels aside. Strain the liquid through a fine-mesh strainer lined with cheesecloth into a bowl.

Continued

Shell half of the mussels, adding the meat to the cooking liquid. Discard the empty shells and any mussels that did not open. Set the remaining mussels aside.

Meanwhile, bring a large pot of salted water to a rolling boil.

Place the garlic in a large cold sauté pan with the olive oil. Bring to a simmer over low heat and cook for about 1 minute, or just until the garlic is soft and translucent; watch carefully to make sure it does not color at all. Add the tomatoes and cook for 5 minutes, stirring occasionally.

Meanwhile, add the pasta to the boiling water and cook until al dente.

Just before the pasta is done, add all of the mussels and their cooking liquid to the tomatoes and olive oil and simmer gently for 2 minutes.

Drain the pasta well in a colander, and shake to remove excess water. Add the pasta to the mussel sauce and stir gently, or combine by moving the pan back and forth to "flip" the pasta in the sauce. Add the parsley.

Serve the pasta on warm plates, spooning the sauce and mussels over the spaghettini.

CAMPOFILONE PASTA WITH LANGOUSTINES

Maccheroncini di Campofilone con gli Scampi

❀ Serves 6

THE WOMEN OF THE TOWN of Campofilone have an international reputation for their pasta-making prowess. Their wheat is top quality. They use farm-fresh eggs instead of water, which give the pasta its golden color, and they leave it to air-dry very slowly. This slow drying, over the course of a few days, is very important: Industrial pasta is dried quickly, using heat, and as a result, it is already partially cooked.

In Le Marche, we used large mantis shrimp for this recipe, but since they are difficult to find here in America, I make the dish with langoustines. As for Campofilone pasta, if you cannot find it at a local gourmet market, there are many Internet sources (see page 223). High-quality angel hair pasta (an artisanal brand) is an acceptable substitute.

2 pounds langoustines (see Sources, page 223)	Kosher salt and freshly ground white pepper
¾ cup extra virgin olive oil	¾ pound Campofilone maccheroncini (or high-quality angel hair pasta)
5 garlic cloves, very thinly sliced	2 tablespoons chopped Italian parsley
3 small fresh red chiles, seeded and finely chopped	24 basil leaves, torn in half
12 plum tomatoes, peeled, halved, seeded, and each half quartered	

To prepare the langoustines, bring a large pot of salted water to a rolling boil. Meanwhile, fill a large bowl with ice water. Blanch the langoustines in the boiling water for 5 seconds. Transfer to the bowl of ice water and chill for 1 minute to stop the cooking, then drain and place on a baking sheet. Separate the tail section from the body of each one (the bodies and shells can be reserved for making stock). Use a pair of scissors to cut down both sides of each tail shell and remove the bottom of the shell. Gently remove the tail meat from the upper shell. Place the meat in a small bowl, cover, and refrigerate.

Continued

Bring another large pot of salted water to a rolling boil.

Meanwhile, heat ¼ cup of the olive oil in a large sauté pan over medium-high heat. Add the langoustines and sauté for about 1 minute, until they are just cooked through. Transfer to a plate and set aside. Discard the oil remaining in the pan.

Pour the remaining ½ cup of the olive oil into the sauté pan and let it warm for 1 minute. Add the garlic, chiles, and tomatoes and sauté for 2 to 3 minutes, until the tomatoes soften and the garlic looks wilted. Remove the sauce from the heat and season to taste with salt and pepper. Set aside in a warm spot.

Add the pasta to the boiling water and cook for about 3 minutes, or until al dente. Drain well.

Meanwhile, bring the sauce just to a simmer over medium-high heat. As soon as it returns to a simmer, add the pasta, langoustines, and parsley. Season to taste with salt and pepper. Fold in the basil leaves, and serve immediately in warm pasta bowls.

BAKED STUFFED MACCHERONI

Boccolotti alla Pesarese

❋ Serves 6

IN MARCHIGIANI DIALECT, large pasta tubes resembling giant rigatoni are known as *boccolotti*. They fairly cry out for stuffing. When I first developed an interest in cooking, long before I went to cooking school, this was one of the first dishes I tried to make at home. My sister, Claudia, and I would unfailingly create a truly big mess in the kitchen. But I was determined to get it perfect, so I made it again and again until it seemed right to me. Claudia would laugh at how determined I was. To her, it was a lark. To me, it was a serious matter.

The mix of veal, chicken, prosciutto, wild mushrooms, chicken livers, fresh cream, and cheese bursts with flavor. If you are lucky enough to have them, you could use truffles instead of mushrooms. Some might find it painstaking to stuff pasta like this, one by one, but anyone who likes to get into a "cooking trance" will find it a peaceful and pleasurable process, as I do.

Pasta

1 pound (or 500 g) extra-large rigatoni (see Sources, page 223)

6 tablespoons extra virgin olive oil

Stuffing

3½ tablespoons unsalted butter

2 shallots, minced

½ pound prosciutto, cut into ¼-inch dice

3 ounces wild mushrooms or black truffles, cleaned and cut into ¼-inch dice

½ pound veal loin, cut into ¼-inch dice

½ pound boneless, skinless chicken breasts, cut into ¼-inch dice

⅓ pound chicken livers, cleaned and cut into ¼-inch dice

¾ cup dry Marsala

Kosher salt and freshly ground white pepper

½ cup freshly grated Parmigiano-Reggiano

½ cup heavy cream

3 large egg yolks

Sauce

2 cups heavy cream

2 cups Chicken Stock (page 214)

1 cup freshly grated Parmigiano-Reggiano (about 4 ounces)

Kosher salt and freshly ground white pepper

Continued

3 tablespoons (1½ ounces) unsalted butter, melted	1 cup freshly grated Parmigiano-Reggiano (about 4 ounces)

FOR THE PASTA

Bring a large pot of salted water to a rolling boil. Cook the rigatoni for about 10 minutes, until al dente. Drain and place in a large bowl. Toss with the olive oil, then spread on a baking sheet to cool. Toss occasionally with a wooden spoon as the pasta cools to prevent sticking.

FOR THE STUFFING

Melt the butter in a large sauté pan over medium-high heat. Add the shallots and prosciutto and cook for 5 minutes, or until the shallots are soft and translucent but not browned. If you are using wild mushrooms, now is the time to add them. Add the veal and chicken and sauté, stirring often, for about 5 minutes, or until the meat has browned. Add the chicken livers and sauté for another 2 minutes.

Add the Marsala and bring to a simmer, scraping the bottom with a wooden spatula or spoon to loosen all the browned bits. Simmer for about 4 minutes, to reduce the wine by one-third. Season to taste with salt and pepper, and transfer the mixture to a food processor.

Add the truffles, if using, and the Parmigiano-Reggiano and process until smooth. With the machine running, add the cream and yolks and process until thoroughly blended.

To check the seasoning, cook a quarter-size patty of the stuffing in a small sauté pan. Adjust the seasoning as necessary. Transfer the stuffing to a covered container and refrigerate for at least 1 hour, or up to 1 day, to blend the flavors.

Position a rack in the center of the oven and preheat the oven to 400°F.

Combine the cream and chicken stock in a medium saucepan and bring to a simmer over low heat. Simmer gently until the liquid is reduced to ⅔ cup. Transfer to a blender. Add the Parmigiano and blend until smooth. Season to taste with salt and pepper. Set aside.

Spoon the stuffing into a pastry bag fitted with a ½-inch plain tip. Pipe the stuffing into the rigatoni, placing the stuffed pasta on a tray.

Using a pastry brush, generously brush a 19½-by-11½-inch gratin dish or other large baking dish with the melted butter. Arrange the stuffed rigatoni in the baking dish. Pour the reduced cream mixture over the top and sprinkle evenly with the Parmigiano.

Bake for 15 minutes, or until the top is lightly browned and bubbling. Serve immediately.

BUCATINI WITH GUANCIALE
Bucatini al Guanciale

WHEN I WAS A BOY, this simple dish was a favorite for lunch at our apartment at number 12 Via Guazzatore. But as recently as a few years ago, I probably would not have included the recipe in a cookbook for use in America, because guanciale, cured hog jowls, were unlikely to be available to home cooks. Now, though, you can buy guanciale in many shops that sell gourmet products, as well as in Italian specialty markets.

Anyone who has attended a pig roast in the American South knows that the cheek is one of the prized parts. Because it is a muscle that gets so much exercise, the meat is rich and succulent. I usually keep some guanciale or pancetta in the refrigerator, ready to fix a quick sauce, to lend robust flavor to beans, to enrich stews. If necessary, you can substitute pancetta for the guanciale here.

½ pound guanciale (see Sources, page 223) or pancetta

1 pound bucatini

1 cup freshly grated Parmigiano-Reggiano (about 4 ounces)

½ cup grated pecorino

Kosher salt and freshly ground black pepper

Bring a large pot of salted water to a rolling boil.

Meanwhile, remove any herbs and spices from the surface of the guanciale and trim away any dry spots. Cut into medium-fine dice. (Or, if using pancetta, cut it into medium-fine dice.) Put the guanciale (or pancetta) in a large sauté pan, place the pan over medium-high heat, and slowly render the fat from the meat. When the guanciale begins to crisp, after 3 to 4 minutes, remove the pan from the heat and set aside.

Add the bucatini to the boiling water and cook until al dente, 8 to 10 minutes.

Meanwhile, return the pan with the guanciale to the stovetop and slowly warm over medium-low heat.

Drain the pasta, reserving about ¼ cup of the cooking liquid. Add the pasta and grated cheese to the guanciale and shake the pan back and forth to combine the ingredients. Add just enough of the reserved pasta water—a few tablespoons should suffice—to create a sauce with a creamy consistency. Season with salt and pepper to taste and serve immediately in warm pasta bowls.

Pappardelle with Wild Boar Ragu

Cinghiale con le Pappardelle

❁ *Serves 6*

DURING WILD BOAR SEASON, my dad's hunter friends would stop by to drop off some meat if they had been blessed with good luck on the boar hunt. Cooked at home, it was great, but I particularly loved the boar at the local grill restaurant. It was well known to hunters, who were welcomed with their game bags, and the owner, Andreina, happily grilled game over a wood fire. Sometimes if I close my eyes, the memory is so strong that I can hear the "*psst psst*" of drops of fat and the wine and rosemary marinade dripping onto the coals as Andreina tended the spit. I still go there every time I am in Le Marche. Note that the meat for the ragu must be marinated overnight.

Ragu

1½ pounds boneless wild boar leg, cut into ¼-inch dice (see Sources, page 223)

1 onion, finely diced

½ cup thinly sliced garlic

2 stalks celery, finely diced

1 medium carrot, finely diced

3 bay leaves, preferably fresh

3 whole cloves

1 bottle (750 ml) dry red wine, such as Montepulciano or Zinfandel

Semolina flour for dusting

Pasta Dough 2 (page 213)

1 cup dried porcini (about 1 ounce)

½ pound (2 sticks) unsalted butter

Kosher salt and freshly ground black pepper

1 tablespoon extra virgin olive oil

¼ pound prosciutto, cut into ¼-inch dice

¾ cup Veal Stock (page 215) or Chicken Stock (page 214)

⅓ cup freshly grated Parmigiano-Reggiano

FOR THE RAGU

Combine the boar, onion, garlic, celery, carrot, bay leaves, cloves, and wine in a large airtight container or resealable plastic bag. Cover or seal, and refrigerate overnight.

FOR THE PASTA

Dust a work surface with semolina. Divide the pasta dough into 4 pieces. One at a time, flatten each piece of dough with the palm of your hand and then roll it through a pasta machine, working from the largest setting to the smallest and rolling it through each setting twice. Lay the completed sheets of pasta on the semolina-dusted work surface and keep covered with a slightly dampened kitchen towel as you work.

Prepare a baking sheet by dusting it with semolina. Using a sharp knife, cut the sheets of pasta crosswise into long ¾-inch-wide ribbons and place on the prepared baking sheet. Cover with a kitchen towel and refrigerate.

TO COOK THE RAGU

Place the porcini in a bowl and cover with warm water. Soak for 30 minutes. Lift out the mushrooms from the soaking liquid (the dirt will have dropped to the bottom of the bowl) and squeeze dry. Chop the mushrooms and place in a small bowl. Strain the liquid through a fine-mesh strainer lined with cheesecloth and pour over the porcini. Set aside.

Drain the meat and vegetables, reserving the marinade; set the meat and vegetables aside. Transfer the marinade to a medium saucepan and bring to a simmer over medium-low heat, skimming the surface frequently.

Meanwhile, melt the butter in a large sauté pan over medium-high heat. Working in small batches, add the boar and vegetables and sauté for about 5 minutes, or until the onions are soft and translucent and the meat is golden brown. Season to taste with salt and pepper, and pour into a colander set over a bowl to drain excess fat.

Add the olive oil to the pan and set over low heat. Add the prosciutto and sauté until golden brown, about 5 minutes. Return the meat and vegetables to the pan, raise the heat to medium-high, and add the marinade. Bring to a boil, scraping the pan with a wooden spatula or spoon to release the browned bits clinging to the bottom. Reduce the heat to medium-low and simmer until the liquid is reduced by two-thirds, about 10 to 12 minutes.

Continued

Add the porcini, with their liquid, and the stock. Partially cover and simmer gently for 2 hours, or until the sauce is the consistency of maple syrup. Season to taste with salt and pepper. Remove from the heat and keep warm.

Meanwhile, bring a large pot of salted water to a rolling boil.

Add the pappardelle to the boiling water and cook until it rises to the surface, stirring from time to time. Drain well, add to the sauté pan, and toss to coat with the sauce. Place in warmed serving bowls, top with the grated Parmigiano, and serve immediately.

LE MARCHE LASAGNE
Vincisgrassi

❁ *Serves 6*

HOW MANY OTHER PEOPLES would name their trademark recipe in honor of the general of an occupying army? We did. Vincisgrassi derives its name from General Windish Graetz, who served with the Austrians in the Napoleonic Wars. The noodles in vincisgrassi are softer and finer than the substantial sheets of pasta that are typical of the lasagne served in America. And while other lasagne recipes call for five layers of noodles, or often only three, ours must have twelve. I can't tell you why this is the case, but I do know that all those smooth, slippery layers of pasta feel so nice on your tongue. The filling can be almost any combination of meat, cheese, and vegetables, but in this somewhat simplified version of the labor-intensive classic—even in Le Marche, it was reserved for special occasions—I left out the organ meats which we always use in Italy but which are less popular in America. I include porcini mushrooms, whose texture complements the noodles very nicely, and I cut the number of layers of pasta down to five. There are truffles too, because vincisgrassi is made in Macerata and in other areas where truffles are abundant, but consider them optional.

Semolina flour for dusting
Pasta Dough 1 (page 212)

Ragu
1 cup dried porcini (about 1 ounce)
1 bay leaf, preferably fresh
1 sprig rosemary
1 sprig thyme
½ pound (2 sticks) unsalted butter
6 ounces prosciutto, cut into ¼-inch dice
3 cups very finely diced onions
1 cup very finely diced celery

1 cup very finely diced carrots
1 tablespoon tomato paste
¼ cup extra virgin olive oil
2½ pounds boneless veal shoulder, trimmed and cut into ¼-inch dice
4 cups dry Marsala
2 cups Veal Stock (page 215)
2 cups Chicken Stock (page 214), or as needed
3 whole cloves
Kosher salt and freshly ground black pepper
5 cups finely chopped white mushrooms

Continued

Béchamel	2 tablespoons (1 ounce) unsalted butter, melted
4 cups heavy cream	
4 cups Chicken Stock (page 214)	2 cups freshly grated Parmigiano-Reggiano (about 8 ounces)
1 large egg	
Kosher salt and freshly ground white pepper	1 to 2 ounces black truffle (optional)

Sprinkle a baking sheet with semolina and set aside. Dust a counter or other work surface lightly with semolina.

Divide the pasta dough into 5 pieces. One at a time, flatten each piece of dough under the palm of your hand and then roll it through a pasta machine, working from the largest setting to the smallest and passing the dough through each setting twice. Use a sharp knife or pastry cutter to cut the sheets of pasta into 13-inch lengths. Lay the completed sheets of pasta on the semolina-dusted counter and keep covered with a slightly dampened kitchen towel as you work.

Bring a large pot of salted water to a rolling boil. Meanwhile, fill a large bowl with ice water. Add enough salt to the water so that it tastes salty. (The salt in the ice water will keep the flavor of salt in the cooked pasta as it cools.)

Add the pasta to the boiling water and cook for 2 minutes. Drain, and immediately submerge the pasta in the ice water.

Line a baking sheet pan with kitchen towels. Drain the pasta and transfer it to the baking sheet, layering it between additional kitchen towels to dry.

FOR THE RAGU

Place the porcini in a bowl and cover with warm water. Soak for 30 minutes.

Lift the mushrooms from the soaking liquid (the dirt will have dropped to the bottom of the bowl), squeeze dry, and chop. Set aside. For a more pronounced mushroom flavor in the dish, strain the liquid through a fine-mesh strainer lined with cheesecloth. Measure the strained liquid and use it in place of some of the chicken stock.

Tie the bay leaf, rosemary, and thyme together with kitchen twine. Set aside.

Melt 8 tablespoons of the butter in a large saucepan over medium-high heat. Add the prosciutto and sauté for 4 minutes, or until golden brown. Add the onions, celery, and carrots, reduce the heat to medium, and cook gently for 10 minutes, or until very soft, watching carefully so the vegetables do not brown. Add the tomato paste and cook for 2 more minutes over medium-low heat, stirring from time to time.

Meanwhile, heat a large sauté pan over medium-high heat. Add the remaining 8 tablespoons butter and 2 tablespoon of the olive oil. Once the butter has melted, add the veal and sauté for about 8 minutes, or until golden brown. Transfer the veal to a colander to drain off the excess fat. Discard the fat in the sauté pan and set the pan aside.

Add the veal to the saucepan with the vegetables. Set aside.

Return the pan used to sauté the veal to the stovetop and warm over medium-high heat. Add the Marsala and bring to a boil, stirring with a wooden spatula or spoon to loosen all the caramelized bits from the bottom of the pan.

Pour the Marsala into the pan with the veal. Bring to a simmer and reduce the liquid by one-third. Add the veal stock, chicken stock (and mushroom liquid, if using), and cloves and stir well. Add the herb bundle and submerge it in the sauce. Partially cover the pan and let the ragu simmer gently for 2 hours. Remove from the heat, season to taste with salt and pepper, and set aside (discard the herb bundle once the ragu has cooled).

Heat the remaining 2 tablespoons olive oil in a medium sauté pan over high heat. Add the white mushrooms and porcini and sauté for about 5 minutes, or until the white mushrooms are soft and lightly golden. Fold the mushrooms into the ragu; set aside.

FOR THE BÉCHAMEL

Combine the cream and chicken stock in a large saucepan, bring to a simmer, and simmer gently for about 20 minutes, or until reduced to about 2 cups.

Continued

Pour the cream mixture into a blender and blend well, first at low speed, then increasing to medium speed. Blend in the egg. Season with salt and pepper. Strain the sauce through a fine-mesh strainer into a bowl. Cool to room temperature.

Position a rack in the center of the oven and preheat the oven to 350°F.

TO ASSEMBLE THE LASAGNE

Using a pastry brush, coat a 9-by-13-inch baking pan with the melted butter. Lay the first sheet of pasta in the pan.

Sprinkle a generous ⅓ cup of the Parmigiano over the pasta. Ladle or spoon about ¾ cup of the ragu over the pasta and use the back of the ladle or spoon to spread it evenly over the pasta. Spoon about ½ cup béchamel over the ragu and spread it in an even layer. Top with another sheet of pasta. Cover with Parmigiano and continue to layer the ingredients, topping the last sheet of pasta with a layer of béchamel and finishing with Parmigiano.

Place the baking dish on a baking sheet and bake for 25 minutes, or until the sauce is bubbly. Increase the heat to 400°F and bake for an additional 5 minutes to brown and crisp the top. Remove the dish from the oven and let stand for 20 minutes.

Cut the vincisgrassi into squares and serve. If you are feeling particularly festive, top with shaved black truffle.

LE MARCHE RISOTTO
Risotto alla Marchigiana

❋ *Serves 6*

IF YOU SIMPLY SAID "RISOTTO," to any Marchigiano, this is the recipe that would come to mind. There are other traditional Le Marche risottos, made with quail, for example (see page 84), duck, and shrimp, but they are saved for special occasions. This is our "go-to" risotto. Its butter and cheeses make for a rich but not unusual combination that you might easily find anywhere in Italy. What makes it different is the cinnamon, one of the aromatic spices used in our cooking that reflect the long relationship Le Marche had with the seafarers of North Africa and the spice traders of the East. The cinnamon adds a beautiful aroma to the dish. For a little more elaborate version, you can do as my Nonna Palmina did and top it with a classic sugo finto made with tomato paste cooked down with sweated onions (see the recipe on page 210).

12 cups Chicken Stock (page 214), or as needed	¼ cup grated mild pecorino, plus more for serving
12 tablespoons (6 ounces) unsalted butter, softened	¼ cup freshly grated Parmigiano-Reggiano
¼ cup finely chopped onion	¼ teaspoon ground cinnamon
2 ¼ cups Carnaroli or Arborio rice	Freshly ground black pepper
Kosher salt	1 lemon
1¼ cups dry white wine, such as Verdicchio or Pinot Grigio	

In a medium saucepan, bring the chicken stock to a boil. Reduce the heat and keep at a low simmer.

Continued

Melt 2 tablespoons of the butter in a large sauté pan over medium heat. Add the onion, reduce the heat to low, and cook slowly, stirring occasionally with a wooden spatula or spoon, until the onion is soft and translucent but has not browned. Add the rice and 1 teaspoon salt and stir for 1 to 2 minutes to toast the rice. Add the white wine, increase the heat, and simmer, stirring constantly, until the pan is almost dry.

Ladle ½ cup of the simmering stock into the rice and stir constantly until it is completely absorbed. Continue cooking and adding stock ½ cup at a time, stirring constantly and letting each addition be absorbed before adding the next. After about 16 to 18 minutes, you should have added about 10 cups stock, the rice should be al dente, and the risotto should be quite thick and creamy. If the rice is not yet al dente, add more stock and continue cooking as necessary.

Remove the pan from the heat and gently fold in both cheeses, the remaining 10 tablespoons butter, and the cinnamon. The risotto should be soft and creamy. If it seems too thick, add more stock a spoonful or so at a time. Season to taste with salt and pepper.

Using a Microplane or other fine grater, lightly grate lemon zest over each plate. Top with the risotto, finish with grated pecorino, and serve immediately.

SCORPION FISH RISOTTO
Risotto con lo Scorfano

❀ *Serves 6*

THE SEAFOOD STANDS in Grottamare in the province of Ascoli Piceno made a beautiful version of this risotto. In the summer we would sometimes drive there for a day at the beach, relaxing under the palm trees and, of course, finishing with a seaside meal.

We normally make this recipe with scorfano, or scorpion fish, a bony Mediterranean fish, but you can use any firm-fleshed white fish, such as striped bass or snapper. One of the principles for getting the most out of fish is proper filleting technique. My teacher in this was Vincenzo Camerucci, who was a master at separating the flesh from the bones so that all that would go into the stock were heads and bones. I worked at his restaurant, Lido, in Cesenatico when I was eighteen. Vincenzo was meticulous, and he had a very developed palate as well. He was one of the first Le Marche chefs to attempt to refine our regional foods, which is why he became one of the few chefs in our region to earn a Michelin star.

NOTE When you buy the fish, make sure to ask the fishmonger to save the heads and bones for you. They will give the broth more flavor.

3 scorpion fish or striped bass, about 2 pounds each, cleaned, scaled, and filleted (have the fishmonger do this), bones reserved

1 cup extra virgin olive oil

2 medium onions, coarsely chopped

2 celery stalks, coarsely chopped

4 garlic cloves, thinly sliced

6 plum tomatoes, coarsely chopped

6 cups dry white wine, such as Verdicchio or Pinot Grigio

Pinch of saffron threads

1 tablespoon crushed white peppercorns

4 quarts Fish Stock (page 217)

2 sprigs Italian parsley

2 basil leaves

2 sprigs chervil

2 sprigs tarragon

Kosher salt and freshly ground black pepper

10⅔ tablespoons (5⅓ ounces) unsalted butter

2 shallots, minced

Continued

2 cups Carnaroli or Arborio rice	3 tablespoons chopped Italian parsley or
1 bay leaf, preferably fresh	1 tablespoon each chopped parsley, chervil, and tarragon

FOR THE STOCK

Run your fingers down the surface of the fillets to check the flesh for pin-bones; remove any bones you find with kitchen tweezers. Rinse the fillets under cool water and pat dry. Cut into 1-inch squares. Transfer to a plate, cover with plastic wrap, and refrigerate.

Remove the gills from each fish head and discard. Use a large chef's knife to cut the heads in half, and cut the backbones into 3 pieces each. Place the head and bones in a colander and rinse thoroughly. Pat dry.

Pour ½ cup of the olive oil into a medium pot and heat over medium-high heat. Add the onions, celery, and garlic and cook, stirring occasionally, for about 6 minutes, or until soft, translucent, and slightly golden. Add the fish heads and bones and sweat for 1 minute. Add the tomatoes and cook until softened, about 8 minutes. Lower the heat if necessary to keep the vegetables from browning.

Add 4 cups of the wine to the pot. Bring to a simmer, scraping with a wooden spatula or spoon to release any browned bits clinging to the bottom of the pot. Simmer until the wine is reduced by half, 8 to 10 minutes. Add the saffron, peppercorns, and fish stock, reduce the heat to medium-low, and bring the stock to a simmer, skimming the surface to remove any residue. Add the parsley, basil, chervil, and tarragon and simmer gently for 25 minutes, skimming the surface as necessary.

Remove the stock from the heat, cover, and let rest for 10 minutes to allow the impurities to sink to the bottom. Carefully ladle the stock through a fine-mesh strainer into a saucepan, disturbing the bones as little as possible to keep the stock clear; tilt the pot, and carefully pour off the last of the stock. Set aside.

Season the fish with salt and pepper. Place the fish skin side down in a large sauté pan in a single layer. Ladle in just enough stock to cover the fish. Set aside.

FOR THE RISOTTO

Melt half of the butter in a large sauté pan over medium heat. Add the shallots, reduce the heat to low, and cook for about 5 minutes, or until soft and translucent but not browned. Add the rice and bay leaf and stir for 1 to 2 minutes to toast the rice. Add the remaining 2 cups wine, increase the heat, and simmer, stirring constantly, until the pan is almost dry.

Ladle enough stock into the pan to cover the rice and stir constantly until it has been absorbed. Continue cooking and adding stock 1 cup at a time, stirring constantly and letting each addition be absorbed before adding the next. After about 16 to 18 minutes, you should have added 10 cups stock, the rice should be al dente, and the risotto should be quite thick and creamy. If the rice is not yet al dente, add more stock and continue cooking as necessary.

Once the rice is al dente, place the sauté pan with the fish over medium-high heat, bring to a simmer, and cook for about 3 minutes, or until the fish is just opaque throughout and firm to the touch.

Meanwhile, add the remaining butter and ½ cup olive oil to the risotto and mix well. Fold in the chopped herbs. The risotto should be soft and creamy. If it seems too thick, add more stock a spoonful or so at a time. Season to taste with salt and pepper.

Transfer the risotto to a large bowl to serve family-style, or spoon into individual serving dishes. Top with the pieces of fish and a bit of the poaching stock. Serve immediately.

QUAIL RISOTTO WITH PROSCIUTTO
Risotto con le Quaglie

❀ Serves 6

WHEN MY ANCESTORS were still country people, Trabocchi men were known for their skill with grilled meats, including a lot of wild game. Old-timers in Osimo still talk about the days when my grandfather would ride into town with his shotgun over his shoulder and two knives stuck in his belt. Back then, the men of our family were known as a tough bunch. . . . But that was before my time. One of their favorite game birds was the quail.

Le Marche is on an ancient flight path for quail. I remember, as a kid, walking with my dad's childhood friend Maria del Brando on her farm when she pointed out some quail to me. I don't think I'd ever enjoyed a game as much as I enjoyed running up to a covey of quail, flapping my arms, and screaming until they all took off at once. Franca Battistelli, Maria's daughter and my father's neighbor today in Osimo, makes the absolute best version of this dish. Hers is the basis for the recipe below.

NOTE Jumbo quail are larger and meatier than ordinary quail, weighing about 5 to 7 ounces each. They are available from specialty butchers or through mail-order (see Sources, page 223).

Quail

¼ cup dried porcini

6 jumbo quail (see Note)

Kosher salt and freshly ground black pepper

Six 2-inch sprigs rosemary

6 garlic cloves

8 tablespoons (4 ounces) unsalted butter

¼ cup very finely diced carrot

¼ cup very finely diced celery

¼ cup very finely diced onion

⅓ cup very finely diced prosciutto

2 cups dry red wine, such as Montepulciano or Zinfandel

Risotto

12 cups Chicken Stock (page 214), or as needed

8 tablespoons (4 ounces) unsalted butter

¼ cup minced shallots

1 ¾ cups Carnaroli or Arborio rice

1 bay leaf, preferably fresh

2 cups dry white wine, such as Verdicchio or Pinot Grigio

½ cup freshly grated Parmigiano-Reggiano

½ cup grated mild pecorino

FOR THE QUAIL

Place the porcini in a bowl and cover with warm water. Soak for 30 minutes.

Lift the mushrooms from the soaking liquid (the dirt will have dropped to the bottom of the bowl), squeeze dry, and chop. Set aside. For a more pronounced mushroom flavor in the dish, strain the liquid through a fine-mesh strainer lined with cheesecloth. Measure the strained liquid and use it in place of some of the chicken stock.

Meanwhile, season the cavities of the quail with salt and pepper. Place 1 sprig of rosemary and 1 garlic clove in each cavity. Lightly season the outside of each quail with salt and pepper. Place on a plate, cover, and let stand at room temperature for 30 minutes.

Position one oven rack in the upper third of the oven and the other one in the lower third. Preheat the oven to 400°F.

Heat two large ovenproof sauté pans over medium heat (see Note). Melt 4 tablespoons of the butter in each pan. Once the butter has melted, place 3 quail in each pan and brown on all sides until the birds have an overall golden color, about 5 to 6 minutes total. As they cook, tilt the pans from time to time and use a large spoon to baste the birds with butter. Transfer the birds to a platter and set aside.

Combine the carrot, celery, and onion in a small bowl, then add half of the vegetables to each sauté pan. Cook over low heat about 5 minutes, or until soft and translucent. Add half the prosciutto to each pan and sauté for 1 minute. Add 1 cup of the red wine to each pan and bring to a simmer, using a wooden spatula or spoon to scrape up all the brown bits clinging to the bottom of the pan. Return the quail to the pans and scatter the porcini mushrooms around them.

Continued

Transfer the sauté pans to the oven and roast the quail for about 15 minutes, until the breast meat is cooked to medium. Transfer the quail to a plate and cover with aluminum foil. Let rest for 10 minutes in a warm corner of the kitchen.

WHILE THE QUAIL ROAST, COOK THE RISOTTO

In a medium saucepan, bring the chicken stock to a boil. Reduce the heat and keep at a low simmer.

Melt 4 tablespoons of the butter in a large sauté pan over medium heat. Add the shallots, reduce the heat to low, and cook for about 5 minutes, until soft and translucent but not browned. Add the rice and bay leaf and stir for 1 to 2 minutes to toast the rice. Add the white wine, increase the heat, and simmer, stirring constantly, until the pan is almost dry.

Ladle 1½ cups of the simmering stock into the rice and stir constantly until it is completely absorbed. Continue cooking and adding stock 1 cup at a time, stirring constantly and letting each addition be absorbed before adding the next. After about 16 to 18 minutes, you should have added about 10 cups stock, the rice should be al dente, and the risotto should be quite thick and creamy. If the rice is not yet al dente, add more stock and continue cooking as necessary.

Remove the pan from the heat and gently fold in both cheeses and the remaining 4 tablespoons butter. The risotto should be soft and creamy. If it seems too thick, add more stock a spoonful or so at a time. Season to taste with salt and pepper.

Divide the risotto among six warm plates. Place 1 quail on each plate of risotto. Spoon a few tablespoons of the cooking juices and the vegetables over each quail and serve immediately.

NOTE If you don't have ovenproof sauté pans, brown the quail as directed, then transfer the sauce, quail, and mushrooms to a large roasting pan and then to the oven, as above.

Fish and

Shellfish

Langoustines with Fried Cauliflower and Tomato Sauce
Scampi al Pomodoro

❋ *Serves 6*

My father had a friend in San Benedetto who sold fish, so we could always count on buying some great langoustines from him for our Christmas dinner. I loved looking at the display of fresh fish and shellfish: lobsters, branzini, scorpion fish, mullet, clams, and mussels, all sleek and shiny on top of mounds of glistening ice. This combination of seafood with fried cauliflower may seem unusual, but it was actually perfectly logical, because we could always find cauliflower at Christmastime. If langoustines are not available, you can make the dish with shrimp. Or feel free to substitute crayfish, or even lobster tails.

---

36 langoustines (see Sources, page 223) or large shrimp

1 medium cauliflower, cored and separated into florettes

1¼ cups Italian 00 flour or all-purpose flour

1½ teaspoons baking powder

Kosher salt and freshly ground white pepper

3 large eggs

1¼ cups sparkling water, such as Pellegrino

Grated zest of 1 lemon

3 quarts sunflower or peanut oil

¾ cup Basic Tomato Sauce (page 210)

Two 3-inch sprigs mint, leaves removed and chopped

½ cup extra virgin olive oil

FOR THE LANGOUSTINES OR SHRIMP

If using langoustines, bring a large pot of salted water to a rolling boil. Meanwhile, fill a large bowl with ice water. Blanch the langoustines in the boiling water for 5 seconds. Transfer to the bowl of ice water and chill for 1 minute to stop the cooking, then drain and place on a baking sheet. Separate the tail section from the body of each one (the bodies and shells can be reserved for making stock). Use a pair of scissors to cut down both sides of each tail shell and remove the bottom of shell. Gently remove the tail meat from the upper shell. Place the meat in a small bowl, cover, and refrigerate.

If using shrimp, peel and devein them. Rinse in cool water, drain, and pat dry. Place in a small bowl, cover, and refrigerate.

FOR THE CAULIFLOWER

Bring a large pot of salted water to a rolling boil. Meanwhile, fill a large bowl with ice water. Blanch the cauliflower for about 4 minutes, or until it is tender but still with a little bite. Transfer to the ice water and chill for 1 minute to stop the cooking, then drain and pat dry. Set aside.

Combine the flour, baking powder, and a pinch each of salt and pepper in the bowl of a standing mixer. Using the paddle attachment, mix at low speed for 30 seconds. Add the eggs, sparkling water, and zest and mix for 5 minutes. Transfer the batter to a medium bowl, cover, and let rest at room temperature for 10 minutes to 30 minutes.

In a deep fryer or a large deep pot, heat the sunflower oil to 350°F.

Meanwhile, in a small saucepan, bring the tomato sauce to a simmer over low heat. Add the mint and remove from the heat. Set aside.

Line a plate with paper towels. Pour the olive oil in a large nonstick frying pan and heat over medium-high heat until hot. Add the langoustine tails (or shrimp) and sear on each side for about 1 minute, or until lightly golden. Transfer to the plate. Set aside in a warm spot.

Line a baking sheet with paper towels. Working in batches, dip the cauliflower in the batter, shake off any excess, and carefully place in the hot oil. Fry for about 4 minutes, or until golden. Transfer to the prepared baking sheet and blot off any excess oil with paper towels.

Spoon about 2 tablespoons of the warm tomato sauce into each of six serving bowls. Place the langoustines on top of the sauce. Serve the fried cauliflower on the side.

Stewed Cuttlefish

Seppie in Umido

"IN UMIDO" MEANS a very gentle braise. While *umido* most often implies an elaborate stew of all sorts of meats cooked in red wine (see page 154), other dishes are cooked using the same technique. For seppie in umido, the cuttlefish is cooked slowly until it becomes extremely tender. With the tomatoes and onions in the sauce, this is almost like a rich fish soup. In Numana, my father would go down to the waterfront when the fishing boats came in to seek out the best cuttlefish for this dish. As is true with fishermen everywhere, of course, if you want a straight answer from them, you have to approach the subject obliquely. Only after a reasonable amount of time spent in conversation could you spring the question and ask for the fish. As soon as he had it, he would go out to Maria del Brando's for the onions and then to our local *consorzio* (co-op) for extra virgin olive oil. In other words, he would spend a whole day driving from place to place to get the best ingredients. If you love food, though, you don't count mileage.

1½ pounds cuttlefish or calamari, cleaned

1 cup extra virgin olive oil, plus more for drizzling

12 oil-packed anchovy fillets

2½ cups finely chopped onions

⅓ cup finely chopped or sliced garlic

2 bay leaves, preferably fresh

1⅔ cups dry white wine, such as Verdicchio or Pinot Grigio

1¼ cups drained and seeded canned tomatoes

Kosher salt and freshly ground black pepper

2 tablespoons finely chopped Italian parsley

If using cuttlefish, cut lengthwise in half. Rinse and pat dry. Cut into ¼-inch dice. If using calamari, separate the tentacles from the bodies. Cut the bodies into ¼-inch rings and cut each tentacle into 3 or 4 pieces.

In a Dutch oven or other large pot, heat ½ cup of the olive oil over medium-high heat. Add the anchovies. Cook, mashing them with the back of a fork, for about 5 minutes, until they break down and slowly melt into the oil. Add the onions, garlic, and bay leaves and cook for about 5 minutes, until the onions are soft and translucent. Add the wine, increase the heat, and bring to a fast simmer, scraping the pan with a wooden spoon or spatula to loosen any browned bits clinging to the bottom. Simmer until the wine is reduced two-thirds.

Add the cuttlefish and tomatoes, crushing the tomatoes with your hands as you add them, and reduce the heat to a gentle simmer. Partially cover the pot and cook for 35 minutes. Take a test bite: If the cuttlefish is tender, the stew is ready; if not, continue to cook the fish for 5 to 15 minutes longer.

Season to taste with salt and pepper. Ladle into warm bowls. Garnish each with chopped parsley and a drizzle of olive oil.

POLENTA WITH SHELLFISH AND TOMATO SAUCE
Polenta al Sugo di Pesce

In America, pasta is often the thing the home chef makes when he or she is in a hurry. Although we Italians love our pasta too, we are often more likely to make a spur-of-the-moment meal from polenta, especially during the colder winter months. And, of course, when times were hard, polenta was a cheap but filling dish—classic comfort food. Whatever you can put on pasta, you can put on polenta, which I think of as Macerata soul food. I make the polenta a little on the soft side, and serve it in bowls with the fish on top.

NOTE You will need a large pot to cook the sauce with all of the seafood. I like the Le Creuset bouillabaisse pan of enameled cast iron, which has a large capacity and, because it is very heavy, ensures very even cooking.

Polenta
2½ cups water

1 cup white polenta flour (such as Moretti bramati bianca; see Sources, page 223) or finely ground yellow polenta

½ cup extra virgin olive oil

Kosher salt and freshly ground black pepper

Sauce
½ cup plus 2 tablespoons extra virgin olive oil

1½ cups finely chopped onions

3 garlic cloves, thinly sliced

1 small fresh red chile, seeded and minced

½ pound clams, scrubbed

½ pound mussels, scrubbed and debearded

¾ cup dry white wine, such as Verdicchio or Pinot Grigio

12 prawns, head on, or large shrimp, preferably head on, peeled and deveined

½ pound cleaned calamari, cut into ½-inch dice

8 plum tomatoes, peeled, seeded, and cut into ¼-inch dice

Kosher salt and freshly ground black pepper

¼ cup finely chopped Italian parsley

¼ cup basil leaves, torn into pieces

Before beginning the polenta, have all of the tomato sauce and shellfish ingredients ready to cook.

FOR THE POLENTA

Pour the water into a heavy pot and bring to a simmer over medium-high heat. Whisking constantly, add the polenta in a slow, thin stream. Continue whisking until the mixture begins to boil. Exchange the whisk for a wooden spatula or spoon and reduce the heat to low. Stir for 1 minute, then partially cover and cook for 45 minutes, until the polenta is very creamy and about the consistency of loose mashed potatoes. Check often and stir well every 5 to 10 minutes to make sure the polenta does not stick to the bottom of the pot.

ABOUT 15 MINUTES BEFORE THE POLENTA IS DONE, START THE SAUCE

Pour ½ cup of the olive oil into a large pot, add the onions, garlic, and chile, and place over medium-high heat. Stir occasionally until the onions and garlic start to sizzle. Reduce the heat to medium, to prevent browning, and cook for about 5 minutes, or until the onions are soft and translucent.

Increase the heat to high, add the clams, mussels, and wine, and cover with a tight-fitting lid. Cook for 4 to 5 minutes, or until the clams and mussels begin to open. Add the prawns and calamari, cover, and cook for about 4 minutes longer, until the prawns are just cooked through.

While the seafood is cooking, combine the remaining 2 tablespoons olive oil and the tomatoes in a medium sauté pan and cook over high heat, moving the pan back and forth on the burner or stirring occasionally, for 3 minutes, or until the tomatoes soften. Season to taste with salt and pepper.

Add the tomatoes to the seafood and cook for 3 minutes to blend the flavors.

Meanwhile, remove the polenta from the heat, stir in the olive oil, and season to taste with salt and pepper.

Remove the sauce from the heat, sprinkle with the parsley and basil, and season to taste with salt and pepper. Spoon the polenta into warm bowls and ladle the seafood on top. Serve immediately.

MIXED GRILL OF FISH AND SHELLFISH
Grigliata Mista di Pesci

❉ Serves 6

OF THE MANY TECHNIQUES I learned from Ennio Mencarelli, none was more challenging than grilling fish over hot coals. This may sound simple enough, but creating a good hot fire that cooks but does not burn is an art. When I messed up on my fire building, everyone in earshot would hear Ennio's loud and colorful words of displeasure.

Today I particularly enjoy making this dish of grilled seafood at home on Sunday. My daughter, Alice, and I go to the fish market and I will let her help pick out the fish. For this recipe, I prefer fish on the bone, which is the way we always grilled in Le Marche. You can use fillets, in which case the cooking time will be much faster, but grilling the whole fish keeps the flesh moister and more flavorful.

Bread Crumbs

2¾ cups dried bread crumbs

1 garlic clove, coarsely chopped

1 cup finely chopped Italian parsley

½ cup extra virgin olive oil

Kosher salt and freshly ground white pepper

Fish and Shellfish

6 medium prawns, heads on, or large shrimp, preferably heads on, peeled and deveined

6 sea scallops, preferably diver scallops, shelled

3 orata (dorade), about 1 pound each, cleaned and scaled

3 branzino or other small white-fleshed fish (see headnote, page 105), about 1 pound each, cleaned and scaled

½ cup extra virgin olive oil

Kosher salt and freshly ground white pepper

Salsa Verde

2 cups finely chopped Italian parsley

1 tablespoon drained and rinsed capers

3 oil-packed anchovy fillets, finely chopped

1 tablespoon finely chopped onion

2 tablespoons dry white wine, such as Verdicchio or Pinot Grigio

1 tablespoon white wine vinegar

½ cup extra virgin olive oil

Kosher salt and freshly ground white pepper

Canola oil

FOR THE BREAD CRUMBS

Combine the bread crumbs, garlic, and parsley in a food processor. While the processor is running, add the olive oil in a slow, steady stream, processing until it is completely absorbed. Season to taste with salt and pepper and process to mix thoroughly. Check the seasoning, then transfer to a bowl and set aside.

FOR THE FISH

Prepare a charcoal grill or preheat a gas grill.

Pat dry the prawns and scallops. If the muscle is still attached, remove it from the side of each scallop.

Place all of the shellfish and fish on a large tray and massage the skin with the olive oil. Season the shrimp and scallops with salt and pepper on both sides, and season the orate and branzino inside and out with salt and pepper. Cover with plastic wrap and refrigerate for 10 minutes.

MEANWHILE, PREPARE THE SALSA VERDE

Combine the parsley, capers, anchovies, onion, wine, and vinegar in a food processor and process to a coarse paste. Scrape the sides of the bowl and process for 2 minutes. While the processor is running, add the olive oil in a slow, steady stream, processing until the oil is fully incorporated. Season to taste with salt and pepper. Transfer the salsa verde to a serving bowl, cover, and refrigerate.

When the fire is very hot, clean the grill grate with a wire brush. Lightly rub (use an old kitchen towel folded in thirds) or brush the grate with canola oil.

Continued

Place the orate and branzino on the grill and cook over medium-high heat for 6 minutes. If they begin to char too quickly, move to a cooler part of the grill or lower the heat. Turn the fish, sprinkle some of the bread crumbs on top, and grill for an additional 6 minutes. Insert a small knife into the thickest part of a fish and examine the flesh closest to the bone; if it is warm and opaque, the fish is cooked. Transfer to a serving platter and set aside.

Meanwhile, grill the prawns for 4 to 6 minutes, turning once halfway through grilling. Grill the scallops over high heat (make sure the grate is very clean, or the scallops may stick) for about 5 minutes, turning once. (If your grill is not large enough, cook the fish first and cover loosely to keep warm, then cook the prawns and scallops.) Remove from the grill and sprinkle with the remaining bread crumbs.

Transfer the prawns and scallops to the serving platter. Serve accompanied by the salsa verde.

Baked Mackerel

Sgombri Arrosto

❊ *Serves 6*

MACKEREL IS ONE OF THOSE FISH that makes some people turn up their noses, saying it is "too fishy." What they are referring to is the smell that fish like mackerel and bluefish get when they've been out of the water for a while. Because these fish are so rich in fish oil (which is very healthful, by the way), you will get that telltale smell unless they are absolutely fresh. But when perfectly fresh, they have much fuller flavor than white-fleshed fish. Here on the East Coast, there are two runs of mackerel each year, signaling the arrival and departure of warm weather.

---

6 mackerel, about 12 ounces each, cleaned, filleted, rinsed, and patted dry

2 cups dry white wine, such as Verdicchio or Pinot Grigio

¼ cup loosely packed mint leaves

2 garlic cloves, coarsely chopped

1⅓ cups dried bread crumbs

1 cup extra virgin olive oil, plus more for the fish

Kosher salt and freshly ground white pepper

8 bay leaves, preferably fresh

Arrange the fillets in a large baking dish, skin side down. Douse with the wine. Cover with plastic wrap and refrigerate for 1 hour.

Preheat the oven to 350°F.

Combine the mint, garlic, bread crumbs, and ⅔ cup of the olive oil in a food processor and process to a smooth paste, about 5 minutes, stopping occasionally to scrape the sides of the bowl. Season to taste with salt and pepper.

Remove the fillets from the marinade (discard the wine) and pat dry. Season with salt and pepper. Massage olive oil into the flesh, using a small pastry brush or your fingers.

Continued

Pour the remaining ⅓ cup oil into a baking dish large enough to hold 6 of the fillets in a single layer. Crush the bay leaves in your hand, and add to the dish. Place half of the fillets in the baking dish, skin side down. Cover them with the bread crumb mixture. Lay the remaining fillets on top, skin side up.

Cover the baking dish with aluminum foil. Bake for about 20 minutes, or until the fish is opaque and the flesh is firm to the touch. Remove from the oven and serve on warm plates, arranging one "stack" of fillets on each plate.

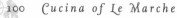

Grilled Dover Sole

Sogliole in Gratella

❀ *Serves 6*

WHILE I LIKE TO SUGGEST substitutes for hard-to-find ingredients, there is no substitute for Dover sole. The delicacy of its flesh is incomparable, yet its flavor is as deep as lobster. To prepare it as we do in Le Marche does not require anything elaborate, just simple respect for the unique qualities of the fish. The elements of this dish are few but important: the freshest sole, the best extra virgin olive oil, and careful attention to the cooking so that the flesh reaches the point of flakiness and no more.

You can find Dover sole (or special-order it) in good fish markets. Ask the fishmonger to remove the head but leave the tail attached. You may also have him remove the skin, but leave the fish on the bone.

---

6 Dover sole, about 1 pound each

2 lemons

¾ cup extra virgin olive oil

2 tablespoons finely chopped Italian parsley

Kosher salt and freshly ground white pepper

Canola oil

About 1 cup seasoned coarse dry bread crumbs (see Note)

Prepare a charcoal fire or preheat a gas grill.

Zest the lemons using a Microplane or other fine grater; you should have about 2 tablespoons zest. Cut the lemons in half and squeeze the juice through a fine-mesh strainer into a small bowl. Whisking constantly, slowly add ¼ cup plus 2 tablespoons of the olive oil. Whisk in the parsley and lemon zest and season to taste with salt and pepper. Cover and set aside.

Using a pastry brush, lightly coat the sole with olive oil. Wrap the tail of each fish with aluminum foil. Season lightly with salt and pepper.

Continued

When the fire is very hot, clean the grill grate with a wire brush. Lightly rub (use an old kitchen towel folded in thirds) or brush the grate with canola oil. Place the fish on the grill, lighter colored side down, and grill about 7 minutes, or until golden brown. Using a spatula, carefully turn the fish and grill for an additional 7 minutes, or until just opaque throughout. Transfer to a platter and let rest in a warm place, covered with foil, for 3 to 4 minutes.

Remove and discard the pieces of foil, and place the fish on warm serving plates. To remove the top 2 fillets from each sole, run a table knife along the center bone, working it toward the edges of one fillet. Repeat on the other side, then remove each fillet carefully with a long spatula and set on a plate. Remove the bones and discard. Then place the top fillets over the bottom ones to re-form the fish. Drizzle a little of the lemon dressing over each fish and sprinkle with bread crumbs and a little salt.

NOTE To make coarse dry bread crumbs, remove the crust from a day-old loaf of country bread. Break up the bread and place in the food processor. Pulse until coarsely ground, with no pieces more than ⅛ inch. Toss the crumbs in a light coating of olive oil and season lightly with salt and pepper. Spread on a baking sheet and bake in a 350°F oven for about 10 minutes, or until golden brown and crisp. Store in an airtight bag.

BAKED RED MULLET STUFFED WITH PROSCIUTTO AND SAGE

Trigle al Prosciutto

❋ *Serves 6 as a light entrée or an appetizer*

MY AUNT LINA had a laugh that filled the street. She was always in charge of making this recipe, and when I was small, she saw that I was interested in learning about it and so she let me help. She would place the fish in the baking dish and I would lay the slices of prosciutto on the white flesh. I can now confess that whenever I helped Aunt Lina, we used a lot of prosciutto because my routine was to eat a slice of prosciutto almost every time I placed another piece on the fish. If any of the dinner guests asked for an extra slice of prosciutto, Lina would cover for me and say that it had all gone into preparing the mullet.

Red mullet is a small delicate fish popular in Europe, especially around the Mediterranean. It is available in some fish markets and through mail-order (see Sources, page 223).

Kosher salt and freshly ground white pepper

12 red mullet fillets, skin on

1 lemon, halved

1¾ cups seasoned dry bread crumbs (see Note, page 102)

½ cup extra virgin olive oil, plus more for sprinkling

6 thin slices prosciutto

6 sage leaves

Sprinkle a large plate with salt and pepper. Arrange the fish skin side down on the plate. Season the flesh lightly with salt and pepper, and squeeze the lemon over the fish. Cover and refrigerate for 1 hour.

Preheat the oven to 425°F. Oil a baking dish large enough to hold 6 of the fillets in a single layer.

Place the bread crumbs in a shallow bowl. Stir in half of the extra virgin olive oil and season with salt and pepper. Cut the prosciutto into pieces about the size of the fillets.

Continued

Lay 6 fillets skin side down in the baking dish. Sprinkle the fillets with olive oil and place a slice of prosciutto and a sage leaf on top of each fillet. Top with the remaining fillets, skin side up. Drizzle with olive oil and sprinkle the bread crumbs over the pairs of fillets.

Roast for 12 to 15 minutes, or until the fish is opaque throughout and firm to the touch. Serve immediately.

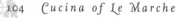

MEDITERRANEAN SEA BASS IN SPICY TOMATO SAUCE

Branzino in Salsa Piccante

BRANZINO IS a small Italian sea bass. That seems a simple enough statement, but the name sea bass means different things in different places. In the northeastern United States, it refers to a bottom-dwelling fish that is often served steamed with soy and garlic in Chinese restaurants. The closest thing here to our branzino is striped bass, but it is hard to find stripers this small unless you buy farm-raised fish; I prefer wild fish. Happily, fresh branzino is becoming more available in big city markets. If you cannot find it, any firm-fleshed white roundfish will do—such as yellowtail, red snapper, or weakfish.

What makes this simple dish so memorable is the wonderful combination of tomatoes, capers, and olives. When I make fish on Sunday afternoons for my family, this is my favorite recipe.

2 branzino or small striped bass, 1¼ pounds each, cleaned, scaled, and heads removed

Kosher salt and freshly ground white pepper

A small bunch of basil, tough stems removed

1½ cups extra virgin olive oil, plus more for drizzling

1 small onion, finely chopped

3 garlic cloves, thinly sliced

1 small fresh thin red chile, finely chopped

1 red bell pepper, cored, seeded, and finely chopped

1 cup dry white wine, such as Verdicchio or Pinot Grigio

3 large ripe tomatoes, peeled, seeded, and chopped

1 tablespoon drained and rinsed capers

¼ cup pitted black olives, such as Kalamata or Taggiasche

2 tablespoons finely chopped Italian parsley

Continued

Preheat the oven to 425°F.

Rinse the fish well and pat dry with paper towels. Season lightly with salt and pepper, inside and out. Stuff each fish with half the basil sprigs. Rub ¼ cup of the olive oil into the skin of the fish. Set aside.

Place a flameproof baking dish or roasting pan large enough to hold the fish comfortably over medium-high heat. Add ¾ cup of the olive oil, the onion, and garlic and sauté for about 5 minutes, or until the onion is very soft and translucent. Add the chile and bell pepper and sauté for 3 minutes, or until softened.

Add the wine, bring to a simmer, and reduce by one-third, about 5 minutes. Reduce the heat to medium-low and add the tomatoes, capers, and olives. When the sauce begins to simmer, remove from the heat and keep warm on the stovetop.

Place a large sauté pan over high heat. Add the remaining ½ cup olive oil and heat until hot. Sear the fish for 3 minutes on each side.

Transfer the fish to the baking dish, and baste with the sauce. Cover tightly with a lid or aluminum foil and bake for 8 minutes. Uncover the pan and increase the oven temperature to 450°F. Bake for about 10 minutes longer, basting every 3 to 4 minutes, until the fish is just cooked through.

Transfer the bass and sauce to a serving platter. Sprinkle with the parsley, drizzle with olive oil, and serve.

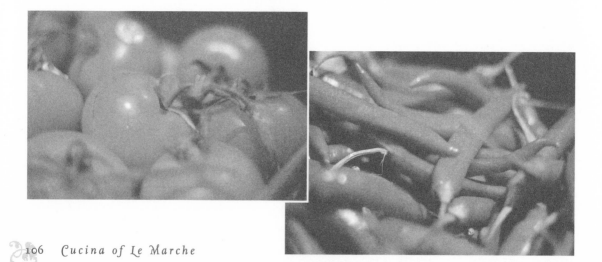

Whiting Ancona-Style

Merluzzo all'Anconetana

MERLUZZO IS ANOTHER one of those fish names that means different things depending on where you are. In Argentina, for example, where there are many descendants of Marchigiani immigrants, merluzzo negro is what North Americans call Chilean sea bass. But that's not what merluzzo meant in Osimo. They were small fish—long and thin—with beautifully delicate white, sweet flesh, much like the whiting available in America. You could buy them more cheaply than more "upscale" fish such as branzino and tonno. Often I would eat two of them and stop only because that's all there was.

You can poach merluzzo, as in this recipe, bake it, sauté it . . . but whatever you do, be gentle. If you overcook it, merluzzo will fall apart.

---

6 whiting, ¾ to 1 pound each, cleaned and scaled

Kosher salt and freshly ground white pepper

¾ cup extra virgin olive oil, plus extra for drizzling

1 small onion, cut into ¼-inch slices

1 garlic clove, minced

1 cup dry white wine, such as Verdicchio or Pinot Grigio

1 pound plum tomatoes, peeled, seeded, and cut into chunks

2 tablespoons finely chopped Italian parsley

Season the whiting lightly with salt and pepper, inside and out. Set aside.

Combine the olive oil, onion, and garlic in a Dutch oven or other heavy pot large enough to hold the fish in one layer. Bring to a simmer over medium-low heat and gently sweat the garlic and onion for about 5 minutes, or until soft and translucent.

Add the wine, increase the heat, and bring to a boil. Cook until reduced by half.

Continued

Add the tomatoes, then lay the fish in the pot. Lower the heat to a simmer, cover the pot, and poach the fish gently for 12 minutes, or until the flesh is easily pierced with the tip of a knife.

Add the parsley and season the sauce to taste with salt and pepper. Serve directly from the pot, or transfer to a deep serving platter. Drizzle with olive oil and serve.

GRILLED ORATA WITH ANCHOVY SAUCE

Orate all'Anconetana con Salsa del Papa

❋ Serves 6

MY FATHER USED TO ENJOY GRILLING orate on our custom-made barbecue, made by my godfather, Mario Belardinelli, who was a metalworker. Mario was a small man for such a hard line of work, but whatever he made lasted a long time.

The marinade—shallots, thyme, bay leaves, and white wine—gently imparts its flavor to the fish. The *salsa del papa*, made with anchovies, bread, vinegar, garlic, and hard-boiled eggs, is a lusty accompaniment.

Orate, dorade in French, is sometimes called sea bass here, or sea bream. Orate is what we called it, and it is starting to show up by that name (or orata) in American markets; see Sources, page 223. If you can't find it by any of its names, tilapia or snapper would be a fine substitute.

6 orata (dorade), snapper, or tilapia fillets, 6 to 8 ounces each, skin on, any pinbones removed

Kosher salt and freshly ground white pepper

1 cup minced shallots

2 bay leaves, preferably fresh

¼ cup finely chopped thyme

1 cup dry white wine, such as Verdicchio or Pinot Grigio

Salsa del papa

3 thick slices white bread, crusts removed

2 tablespoons white wine vinegar

¼ cup dry white wine, such as Verdicchio or Pinot Grigio

3 hard-boiled eggs

10 oil-packed anchovy fillets

1 garlic clove, roughly chopped

¾ cup extra virgin olive oil

Canola oil

Continued

Season the flesh of each fillet lightly with salt and pepper. Sprinkle salt, pepper, and half of the shallots over the bottom of a baking dish large enough to hold the fillets in a single layer. Arrange the fillets skin side down on top of the shallots. Cut or break the bay leaves into pieces and sprinkle over the fillets. Sprinkle the thyme over the fish, carefully pour the wine over and around the fish. Cover with plastic wrap and refrigerate for 2 hours.

Meanwhile, prepare the salsa del papa: In a small bowl, combine the bread, vinegar, and wine and set aside to soak for 10 minutes.

Separate the yolks and whites of the eggs; save the whites for another purpose, or discard.

Squeeze the soaked bread to remove excess liquid. Place the egg yolks in a blender, along with the anchovies, soaked bread, and garlic. Pulse to blend. With the blender running, slowly drizzle in the olive oil, blending until the sauce is the consistency of mayonnaise. Season to taste with salt and pepper and transfer to a sauceboat or serving bowl.

Prepare a charcoal or preheat a gas grill. Or preheat a cast-iron grill pan over high heat.

Remove the fillets from the marinade. Pat dry.

When the grill is hot, clean the grill grate with a wire brush. Lightly rub (use an old kitchen towel folded in thirds) or brush the grate (or the grill pan) with canola oil. Place the fish skin side down on the grill (or in the grill pan) and cook, turning once, for 2 to 3 minutes on each side. Serve immediately, with the salsa del papa on the side.

"Drunken" Tuna Marchigiana-Style

Tonno Briaco alla Marchigiana

SINCE THE BEGINNING of time, tuna has been the favorite local catch of Marchigiani fishermen. Beautifully fresh but strongly flavored tuna marries well with sweet, nutty Marsala wine. Crusty toasted country bread brushed with the trio of vinegar, anchovies, and capers provides tang, saltiness, and crunch. If you are wondering about searing the tuna in lard, it works beautifully because tuna is that rare fish that can benefit from such potent and flavorful ingredients. Where "modern" home cooks prefer to avoid lard, in Le Marche we still count it among the most versatile of ingredients.

4 tablespoons (2 ounces) unsalted butter

4 oil-packed anchovy fillets

3 tablespoons manteca (soft lard; see Sources, page 223)

2½ pounds tuna, cut into 6 steaks about 1 inch thick

3 bay leaves, preferably fresh

2 cups dry Marsala

2 tablespoons finely chopped Italian parsley

1 tablespoon drained and rinsed capers

2 tablespoons fresh lemon juice

Kosher salt and freshly ground white pepper

2 tablespoons extra virgin olive oil

Six ½-inch-thick slices crusty country bread, such as ciabatta

Melt the butter in a small saucepan over low heat. Add the anchovies and mix well with a fork, pressing down on the anchovies until the mixture forms a paste. At first it may look as if the butter won't all be incorporated, but it will. Remove from the heat and set aside.

Continued

Melt the manteca in a large skillet over medium-high heat. Once it is very hot, add the tuna and bay leaves. Sear the tuna for about 2 minutes per side, or until golden brown. Add the Marsala and bring to a boil. Reduce to a simmer, cover, and cook for 3 to 4 minutes, until the tuna is medium-rare. Transfer the tuna to a platter and cover loosely to keep warm.

Remove and discard the bay leaves. Reduce the heat to low, keeping the liquid at a gentle simmer. Add the anchovy butter, parsley, capers, and lemon juice, moving the pan back and forth to blend the mixture into a smooth sauce. Season to taste with salt and pepper, remove from the heat, and set aside in a warm spot.

Heat the olive oil in a large sauté pan over medium-high heat until hot. Add the bread and cook for about 1 minute per side, until golden brown.

Arrange the bread in the middle of a platter. Drizzle some of the sauce on the bread. Place the tuna on the bread, and spoon the remaining sauce over the fish. Serve immediately.

Monkfish with Artichokes, Garlic, and Sage
Coda di Rospo

❀ *Serves 6*

ONE OF MY MENTORS at school, Ennio Mencarelli, used to prepare monkfish whenever a VIP came to visit. His recipe called for clams, tomatoes, potatoes cut into little balls, and wild fennel. The monkfish recipe that follows is based on one I picked up from another one of my teachers, Mauro Uliassi, who now owns Italy's finest seafood restaurant, Uliassi. He dreamed it up when the two of us were working for Silvano Pettinari in Senigallia. So, you see, many of the chefs who influenced me are, in one way or another, part of the story of this dish. I particularly like the firm meatiness of monkfish; it reminds me of lobster.

Ask the fishmonger to remove the dark outer skin from the monkfish and slice the fillet for you.

Juice of 1 lemon

6 medium artichokes

⅔ cup extra virgin olive oil, plus more for the fish

3 garlic cloves, peeled

6 sage leaves

Kosher salt and freshly ground white pepper

⅔ cup dry white wine, such as Verdicchio or Pinot Grigio

4 cups sunflower or peanut oil

2½ pounds monkfish fillet, any dark membrane removed and cut into ½-inch-thick slices

Canola oil

Prepare a charcoal grill or preheat a gas grill. Or preheat a cast-iron grill pan over high heat.

Combine half of the lemon juice and 4 cups water in a large bowl. Working with 1 artichoke at a time, snap off the tough green outer leaves until you reach the tender inner yellow leaves. Lay the artichoke on its side and cut off the inner leaves. Trim the bottom of the stem. Using a paring knife, trim away any tough green spots remaining on the artichoke and stem. Using a

Continued

sharp spoon, scoop out the fuzzy choke and place the artichoke heart in the lemon water.

Cut 3 of the artichoke hearts in half, then slice each half into ⅛-inch strips. Return to the lemon water.

Slice the remaining 3 artichoke hearts into quarters and pat dry. Heat ⅓ cup of the olive oil in a medium saucepan over medium-high heat. Add the quartered artichokes, garlic, and sage and sauté for 3 minutes, or until fragrant. Season to taste with salt and pepper. Add the white wine. Bring to a simmer and gently poach the artichokes for about 5 minutes, or until tender. Remove from the heat and set aside.

In a deep fryer or deep heavy pot, heat the sunflower oil to 350°F.

Meanwhile, pat dry the monkfish. Brush or rub the pieces on both sides with olive oil and season lightly with salt and pepper.

When the grill is hot, clean the grate with a wire brush. Lightly rub (use an old kitchen towel folded in thirds) or brush the grate (or grill pan) with canola oil. Place the monkfish on the grill (or in the pan) and cook for 2 minutes per side. Transfer to a serving platter and set aside in a warm spot.

Line a clean plate with paper towels. Drain the sliced artichokes and pat dry.

Fry the strips in the hot oil for about 3 minutes, until crisp and golden. Transfer to a plate and season with salt. Drizzle the remaining lemon juice over the artichokes.

Warm the reserved artichoke hearts over medium heat. Slowly add the remaining ⅓ cup olive oil, stirring constantly until the sauce thickens and becomes creamy.

Spoon the artichokes and sauce over the monkfish, and garnish with the fried artichokes. Serve immediately.

TROUT WITH BLACK TRUFFLES AND ANCHOVY PESTO
Trota di Visso ai Tartufi e Acciughe

❀ *Serves 6*

VISSO IS A BEAUTIFUL little town near the Nera River where the lucky angler can catch a few trout. Americans don't think of Italy as a trout-fishing destination, but sea trout, or brown trout (*salmo trutta*) are native to Europe, and Italy's mountain streams, which flow through limestone valleys, produce wonderful trout. I was particularly impressed by this preparation of simply grilled fish with a sauce of truffles and anchovies. It is served everywhere in Visso. You don't have to use truffles for the dish to come out beautifully. The anchovies alone will do the trick.

6 trout, ¾ to 1 pound each, cleaned

½ cup extra virgin olive oil, plus more for the fish

Kosher salt and freshly ground white pepper

6 small sprigs thyme

6 small sprigs rosemary

6 oil-packed anchovy fillets, minced

3 ounces black truffle, fresh or preserved in oil (see Sources, page 223; truffle "peelings" are fine)

2 tablespoons finely chopped Italian parsley

Prepare a charcoal fire or preheat a gas grill. Or preheat a cast-iron grill pan over high heat. If using a charcoal grill, sprinkle the coals with wood chips soaked in water, if desired.

Rinse the trout inside and out and pat dry. Brush or rub the skin with olive oil and season lightly with salt and pepper inside and out. Insert 1 sprig of each herb into the cavity of each fish. Place the fish on a plate and refrigerate for 10 minutes.

Continued

Place the anchovies in a small bowl. Slice the truffles with a vegetable peeler or other hand-held truffle slicer or mandoline (see Sources, page 223) and add to the anchovies, along with a pinch of salt. Mash the truffles and anchovies with the back of a fork to form a paste. While continuing to mix, add the olive oil in a slow, thin stream. Transfer the sauce to a small serving bowl and set aside.

Grill the trout for 4 to 6 minutes on each side, paying close attention to the color of the fish and the temperature of the grill. When the fish is done, the skin will be golden and crispy and the flesh will be opaque when checked with the tip of a knife.

Transfer the trout to a serving platter, sprinkle with the parsley, and serve with the sauce on the side.

TURBOT IN SMOKY HAY
Rombo nella Paglia

❃ *Serves 6*

THE RECIPE DOES NOT COME from Le Marche, but the inspiration and the aroma do: It is the smell of burning hay. In the countryside, when hay is burned, you first smell a dampness in the air, then a deeper smokiness. Country people often cooked meats and fowl in smoking hay.

One day I was reminiscing with my sous-chef at Maestro, Stefano Frigerio, who is from Lombardy. The subject turned to the sweet smell of hay and, in the way that aroma can often trigger intense memory, we became ravenous as we recalled the lamb—in hay—that farmers sometimes made. We happened to be standing by the fish station, and a beautiful piece of turbot lay in front of us. One thing led to another, and the result is this dramatic recipe.

While you can sometimes find true (European) turbot in gourmet fish markets, striper and flounder work equally well. If turbot is available, have your fishmonger clean the turbot and then split the fish lengthwise in half through the backbone, leaving the fillets attached to the bone.

N O T E You will need to get clean hay from a local farm.

2 turbot, 2 to 3 pounds each, split lengthwise in half (have the fishmonger do this; see the headnote above)	1 tablespoon finely chopped Italian parsley
4 handfuls clean hay	Kosher salt and freshly ground white pepper
4 sprigs rosemary	8 tablespoons (4 ounces) unsalted butter, or as needed
4 sprigs thyme	Fleur de sel
12 fingerling potatoes	
¾ cup extra virgin olive oil	

Rinse the turbot under cool water and pat dry with paper towels.

Divide the hay between two Dutch ovens or other large heavy pots, and place 2 sprigs of rosemary and thyme in each one. Set one pot aside.

Continued

Nestle the potatoes in the hay in the other Dutch oven, cover, and place over medium-high heat. After approximately 45 minutes, remove the potatoes and, using a cloth napkin to protect your fingers from the heat, peel them. (Cover the pot again so the hay won't continue to smoke.) Place the potatoes in a medium saucepan and mash them with a fork until they form a smooth puree. Fold in ½ cup of the olive oil and the chopped parsley, and season to taste. Cover and set aside in a warm spot (if necessary, reheat the potatoes over low heat just before serving).

Place the second Dutch oven over medium-high heat. While it heats, place two large skillets over medium-high heat and add 4 tablespoons of butter to each skillet. When the butter begins to sizzle, add 1 turbot fillet to each skillet and sear for 3 to 4 minutes on each side, until golden. Baste the fish frequently with the butter as it cooks. Transfer to a platter. Repeat with the remaining fillets, adding more butter to the skillets if needed. Set aside.

When you start to smell smoke coming from the Dutch oven, remove the cover and place the seared fish in the hay. Cover and cook for 8 minutes. Transfer the fish to a platter, cover with aluminum foil, and let rest for 8 minutes. (Cover the pot again until the smoke subsides.)

Transfer the fish to a cutting board and remove the meat from the bone using a fillet knife. Place on a platter, skin side down, and sprinkle with fleur de sel. Top with a drizzle of olive oil, and serve immediately, with the potatoes.

FRIED STUFFED OLIVES ASCOLANA-STYLE (*Olive all'Ascolana*), PAGE 14.

ABOVE: FLATBREAD WITH PROSCIUTTO, MOZZARELLA, ARUGULA, AND TOMATO (*Piadina di Cartoceto*), PAGE 26. TOP RIGHT: FARRO SOUP WITH PECORINO AND PROSCIUTTO (*Minestra all'Antica*), PAGE 36. BOTTOM RIGHT: PASSATELLI IN BROTH (*Passatelli all'Urbinate*), PAGE 42.

TOP: SCORPION FISH
RISOTTO (*Risotto con
lo Scorfano*), PAGE 81.
BOTTOM: LE MARCHE
LASAGNE (*Vincisgrassi*),
PAGE 75.

CAMPOFILONE PASTA WITH LANGOUSTINES (*Maccheroncini di Campofilone con gli Scampi*),
PAGE 65.

TOP: MIXED GRILL OF FISH AND SHELLFISH (*Grigliata Mista di Pesci*), PAGE 96.
BOTTOM: GRILLED ORATA WITH ANCHOVY SAUCE (*Orate all'Anconetana con Salsa del Papa*), PAGE 109.

"DRUNKEN" TUNA MARCHIGIANA-STYLE (*Tonno Briaco alla Marchigiana*), PAGE 111.

TOP: TURBOT IN
SMOKY HAY (*Rombo
nella Paglia*), PAGE
117. BOTTOM:
SALT COD POACHED
IN MILK WITH
POTATOES AND
TOMATOES (*Stocca
all'Anconetana*),
PAGE 119.

SALT COD POACHED IN MILK WITH POTATOES AND TOMATOES

Stocco all'Anconetana

❁ *Serves 6*

FROM THE LATE Middle Ages up to the advent of refrigeration, salt cod was the main type of protein consumed in Le Marche. Today its pungent aroma is sometimes off-putting to consumers who are accustomed to shrink-wrapped, odorless groceries. But if you prepare this fish as my aunt Emilia did every Christmas—long, gentle poaching in milk—it is soothing and delicious.

Salt cod is available in Italian and other ethnic groceries, as well as some fish markets. Look for cod that is white and firm to the touch but not rock-hard, yellow, and overdried. (Note that the cod must be soaked for 4 days.) And, if you can get them, use dry or wild fennel branches to replace the rack in the roasting pan. They will add wonderful aroma and flavor to the dish.

2¼ pounds bone-in salt cod, skin on (see Sources, page 223)

1 cup finely chopped onions

¾ cup finely chopped celery

6 garlic cloves, thinly sliced

12 oil-packed anchovy fillets

Three 4-inch sprigs rosemary, leaves removed and finely chopped

1 cup plus 4 tablespoons extra virgin olive oil

8 plum tomatoes, peeled, seeded, and cut into thin strips

1¾ pounds russet (baking) potatoes, peeled, halved crosswise, and cut lengthwise into 1-inch-thick wedges

1 cup dry white wine, such as Verdicchio or Pinot Grigio, or as needed

1 cup whole milk, or as needed

Place the cod in a large bowl, cover with cool water, and refrigerate. Soak for 4 days, changing the water at least twice a day.

Drain the cod and pat dry. Cut into 3-inch squares, being careful to remove all small bones. Leave the skin on. Set aside.

Continued

In a medium bowl, combine the onions, celery, garlic, anchovies, and rosemary.

Place a small metal rack in a Dutch oven or other heavy pot to prevent the fish from sticking. Arrange half of the cod skin side down on the rack. Top with ½ cup plus 2 tablespoons of the olive oil, half of the onion mixture, and half of the tomatoes.

Arrange the remaining fish skin side down on top of the tomatoes. Top with the remaining ½ cup plus 2 tablespoons olive oil, onion mixture, and tomatoes. Cover the vegetables evenly with the potatoes. Combine the wine and milk and pour over the top. The liquid should cover the potatoes; add more if necessary.

Place the pot over medium-high heat and bring to a boil. Reduce to a simmer, cover, and cook gently for 3½ hours. Do not stir the fish with a spoon, but periodically shake the pot gently back and forth to keep the fish from sticking to the rack.

Remove the lid and cook uncovered for about 30 minutes longer. There should be only ½ to 1 inch of liquid left in the pot and the potatoes should be soft.

Transfer the pot to a warm corner of the kitchen and let rest for 20 minutes.

Serve the cod, vegetables, and braising liquid in warm bowls.

FISH STEW
Brodetto all'Anconetana

EVERY MEDITERRANEAN fishing port has a version of this stew. It was the answer to the question that anyone who fishes for a living finds himself asking: "What do I do with all of the little fish left in the net after I've sold the big fish that they want in the market?" Nowadays big trawlers often discard their "by catch," as these so-called less desirable fish are known, but in the past, nothing in the nets was discarded. In Ancona, the result was this fish soup that we think surpasses the best bouillabaisse. We even have an Institute of Brodetto in Ancona!

The traditional recipe calls for thirteen fish, one for each of those at the Last Supper. So, in the recipe that follows, I have listed thirteen fish (and provided local alternatives for our Mediterranean fish), but feel free to use fewer. However, I would not make brodetto without at least two different finfish, two types of shellfish, and either calamari or octopus.

Make sure to cut all the pieces of fish the same size so that they cook evenly. If some fillets are thicker, add them to the pot first and allow them to cook for a few minutes or so before adding the more delicate pieces. You do not want to overcook the fish. In fact, you want to remove the pot from the heat before the fish is thoroughly done, because it will finish cooking in the warm broth.

---

1 cup extra virgin olive oil

5 garlic cloves, 4 thinly sliced, 1 crushed

1 cup diced (¼-inch) onions

6 ounces cleaned octopus, cut into 1-inch pieces

½ cup dry white wine, such as Verdicchio or Pinot Grigio

¼ cup white wine vinegar

3¼ cups Basic Tomato Sauce (page 210)

6 small red mullet fillets, skin on, cut into 2-inch pieces

6 ounces scorpion fish or striped bass fillet, skinned and cut into 2-inch pieces

½ pound John Dory or tilapia fillets, skinned and cut into 2-inch pieces

6 ounces turbot or flounder fillet, skinned and cut into 2-inch pieces

---

Continued

6 ounces monkfish fillet, any dark
membrane removed and cut
into 1-inch-thick medallions

6 ounces cod fillet, skinned, cut into 2-inch
pieces

1 medium boneless skate wing, skinned
(have the fishmonger do this) and cut
into 2-inch pieces

Kosher salt and freshly ground white pepper

6 ounces cuttlefish, cleaned and cut into
½-inch strips (optional)

30 littleneck or Manila clams, scrubbed

18 mussels, scrubbed and debearded

18 medium shrimp, peeled and deveined

6 ounces calamari, cleaned, bodies cut into
½-inch rings, tentacles cut into 3 or 4
pieces each

Six ½-inch-thick slices crusty country
bread, such as ciabatta

1 garlic clove, crushed

½ cup finely chopped Italian parsley

In a very large Dutch oven or other heavy pot, heat ¾ cup of the olive oil over medium-low heat. Add the sliced garlic and the onions and sauté for about 5 minutes, or until the onions are very soft and translucent. Add the octopus, white wine, and vinegar, and bring to a boil, and reduce the liquid by half. Add the tomato sauce, bring to a simmer, and cook for 5 minutes.

Meanwhile, season all of the fin fish with salt and pepper. Set aside.

Add the cuttlefish to the pot, reduce the heat to low, and cook for 8 to 10 minutes. Add the clams and mussels, cover, increase the heat to medium-high, and cook until they open, about 6 minutes. Transfer the clams and mussels to a bowl and cover to keep warm.

Carefully place all the fin fish in the pot and cook for 8 minutes. Do not stir, or the fish may fall apart. Add the shrimp and calamari, cover, and cook for 4 more minutes. Return the clams and mussels to the pot, remove from the heat, and let stand, covered, for 5 minutes.

Meanwhile, preheat the broiler. Brush the bread on both sides with the remaining ¼ cup olive oil. Toast the bread under the broiler, turning once. Rub the warm slices with the crushed garlic.

Sprinkle the brodetto with the parsley, and serve directly from the pot, with the toasted bread.

Fish Stew with Green Tomatoes, Peppers, and Saffron
Brodetto alla Sanbenedettese

❋ *Serves 6*

THIS IS THE PROVINCE of Ascoli Piceno's version of brodetto, named for San Benedetto, a small southern coastal town very close to Abruzzo. It's a simpler dish than the Brodetto all'Anconetana (page 121), and although some of the same seafood that finds its way to Ancona can be found in the markets of San Benedetto, the green tomatoes, green peppers, crushed red pepper, and saffron make for a dish with more zing than the Anconetana rendition of the stew. Or at least that's what the folks from the southern part of Le Marche say.

For even cooking, try to cut all the fish into pieces that are more or less the same size. If some fillets are thicker, add them to the pot first and allow them to cook for a few minutes or so before adding the more delicate pieces. You do not want to overcook the fish.

1 cup extra virgin olive oil

1 medium onion, finely chopped

4 medium green tomatoes, cut into ¼-inch dice

3 green bell peppers, cored, seeded, and cut into ¼-inch dice

1 tablespoon crushed red pepper flakes

1½ teaspoons saffron threads

½ pound monkfish fillet, any dark membrane removed, and sliced into 6 pieces

½ pound skate wing, skinned and cut into 6 pieces

½ pound branzino or sea bass fillet, skin on, cut into 6 pieces

½ pound orata (dorade) fillet, skin on, cut into 6 pieces

Kosher salt and freshly ground white pepper

12 medium prawns, heads on, or large shrimp, preferably heads on, shelled and deveined

½ pound calamari, cleaned, bodies cut into ¼-inch rings, tentacles cut into 3 to 4 pieces each

1¼ cups dry white wine, such as Verdicchio or Pinot Grigio

3 tablespoons white wine vinegar

¼ cup finely chopped Italian parsley

Place a Dutch oven or other large heavy pot over medium-high heat. Add the olive oil and onion and cook for about 5 minutes, or until the onion is soft and translucent. Increase the heat to high, add the tomatoes, green peppers, crushed red pepper, and saffron, and sauté for about 10 minutes, stirring occasionally.

Season all the fish lightly with salt and pepper. Reduce the heat to medium and carefully lay all the fish in the pot. Place the prawns and calamari on top. Increase the heat to medium-high and add the white wine and vinegar. Cover and cook for about 8 minutes, or until the fish is opaque and firm to the touch.

Garnish with the chopped parsley and serve family-style.

Poultry

CHICKEN WITH ROSEMARY, GARLIC, AND TOMATO SAUCE

Pollo in Potacchio

❋ *Serves 6*

POTACCHIO REFERS to any Le Marche dish cooked with tomato, onions, garlic, and rosemary. Chicken is the potacchio that we had most often in my home. Our chickens came from our friend Maria del Brando, whose birds were as good as any organic free-range chicken that you can buy today. Their flesh was a beautiful pale yellow and the skin was dry. When I was six years old, Maria decided I was tall enough to hold the fresh-killed chicken by the feet while she stripped off the feathers. I was so proud!

Back then, everyone knew that a heavy cast-iron skillet was the best way to cook with even overall heat. I still use cast iron in Maestro. If I had to trim my kitchen equipment down to one pan, that would be my pick.

For this dish, the chicken is seasoned with salt, pepper, and rosemary and allowed to marinate so the fragrant herb can permeate the flesh.

1 organic chicken, cut into 10 pieces (see Note)	2 garlic cloves, skin left on, crushed
Kosher salt and freshly ground white pepper	2 cups Basic Tomato Sauce (page 210)
5 sprigs rosemary	4 cups dry white wine, such as Verdicchio or Pinot Grigio
¼ to ½ cup extra virgin olive oil	About ½ cup Chicken Stock (page 214; optional)
1 medium onion, finely chopped	

Lightly season the chicken with salt and pepper. Place the chicken and rosemary in a sealed container or resealable bag. Refrigerate for at least 6 hours, or up to overnight.

Thirty minutes before cooking, remove the chicken from the refrigerator. Reserve the rosemary.

Place a large deep cast-iron skillet that has a lid, or a Dutch oven, over medium-high heat. Add ¼ cup of the olive oil and heat until hot. Working in 2 batches, sear the chicken for 4 to 5 minutes per side, or until golden brown. Transfer to a plate. If necessary, add up to another ¼ cup olive oil between batches.

Add the onion and garlic to the pan. Sauté for 3 minutes, stirring occasionally and pressing down on the garlic cloves. Pour in the tomato sauce and stir constantly for 2 minutes.

Add the wine, scraping the caramelized bits from the bottom of the pan with a wooden spatula or spoon. Reduce the heat to low and return the chicken to the pan. Partially cover the skillet with the lid and braise the chicken for 40 minutes, stirring occasionally. If the pan looks dry at any time, reduce the heat slightly and add some chicken stock or water.

Add the rosemary and cook for an additional 20 minutes, or until the chicken is fork-tender. Transfer the chicken and sauce to a platter and serve.

NOTE Cut the chicken into 2 legs, 2 thighs, 2 wings, and 4 breast pieces.

POTATO GNOCCHI WITH DUCK RAGU
Gnocchi con la Papera

❋ Serves 6

ALL ITALIANS, whether they come from Piemonte, or Tuscany, or Le Marche, have an opinion on properly made gnocchi, and that opinion usually is that their hometown gnocchi is by far the best.

In our house it fell to me to pick the duck for the ragu that would be served with the gnocchi for our big Sunday lunch. On Friday or Saturday we would drive out to Maria del Brando's farm. I would go into the fields with her and pick out a duck. I was quite aware that my choice represented a tragedy for the duck, so I considered the fate of our main ingredient as seriously as a judge at a murder trial. Maria would look at me and laugh.

For the ragu, the duck is cut into pieces and seared, then slowly simmered in the ragu until the sauce is intensely flavorful. In Le Marche, the pieces of duck are then served on a platter with the gnocchi and sauce. However, you can also remove the duck meat from the bones and return it to the rich sauce, to be spooned over the gnocchi.

Gnocchi

2¼ pounds russet (baking) potatoes (all about the same size for even cooking), scrubbed

¾ cup Italian oo flour or all-purpose flour

¼ cup freshly grated Parmigiano-Reggiano

¼ teaspoon freshly grated nutmeg

1 teaspoon kosher salt

3 large egg yolks

Sauce

½ cup dried porcini

1 duck, about 4½ pounds, cut into 12 pieces: thighs, drumsticks, wings, and breasts, each half breast cut into 3 pieces (you can have the butcher do this)

3 tablespoons extra virgin olive oil

¼ pound pancetta, cut into ¼-inch dice

¾ cup finely diced carrots

¾ cup finely diced onion

½ cup finely diced celery

4 cups dry red wine, such as Montepulciano or Zinfandel

2¼ cups Basic Tomato Sauce (page 210)

1 sprig rosemary

1 sprig thyme	Kosher salt and freshly ground black
1 sprig sage	pepper
1 bay leaf, preferably fresh	½ cup freshly grated Parmigiano-
3 whole cloves	Reggiano

FOR THE GNOCCHI

Place the potatoes in a large saucepan with enough cold water to cover. Bring to a boil, then reduce to a simmer and cook for about 45 minutes, or until the potatoes are soft. Drain.

Using a kitchen towel to protect your hands, peel the potatoes while they are still warm. Pass them through a fine drum sieve or a ricer, and spread them evenly on the countertop or a pastry board. Sprinkle the flour, Parmigiano, nutmeg, and salt evenly over the potatoes. Put the egg yolks in the center and, using your hands, mix the flour and other ingredients into the potatoes, working from the outside to the center. Knead the mixture just until a dough forms. (Avoid overworking the dough; the secret to light gnocchi is to handle the dough as little as possible.)

Cover the dough with a dampened kitchen towel and let rest for 30 minutes.

Dust a baking sheet with flour. Sprinkle flour on your work surface. Pull off a small portion of dough and roll it under the palm of your hands until it forms a long narrow cylinder about ¾ inch in diameter. With a sharp knife, cut the dough into ½-inch pieces. Pressing gently, roll each piece down a gnocchi paddle or the back of a kitchen fork to form the characteristic ridges. Place the gnocchi in a single layer on the prepared pan, and repeat with the remaining dough. Cover the gnocchi with cheesecloth or a kitchen towel and refrigerate for up to 6 hours, or freeze for longer storage. (To freeze the gnocchi, let freeze on the baking sheet until firm, then transfer to an airtight container; do not thaw before cooking.)

Continued

FOR THE SAUCE

Place the porcini in a small bowl, cover with warm water, and let soak for 30 minutes.

Meanwhile, season the duck on all sides with salt and pepper. In a large heavy sauté pan, heat 2 tablespoons of the olive oil over medium-high heat. Working in 2 to 3 batches, sear each piece of duck on all sides until golden brown. Set aside.

Drain any excess fat from the pan and return it to medium heat. Add the remaining 1 tablespoon oil to the pan. Add the pancetta and cook until it has rendered its fat and is crisp. Add the carrots, onion, and celery, reduce the heat to medium, and cook gently until the onion and celery are soft and translucent. Add the wine, increase the heat to high, and bring to a simmer, scraping the bottom of the pan with a wooden spatula or spoon. Cook for 10 to 12 minutes, or until the liquid has reduced by two-thirds.

While the liquid is reducing, lift the mushrooms from the soaking liquid and squeeze dry. Chop the mushrooms and set aside. For a more pronounced mushroom flavor in the sauce, strain the soaking liquid through a cheesecloth-lined strainer. Set aside.

Stir the porcini, porcini liquid, if using, and tomato sauce into the pancetta mixture. Add the duck, nestling it in the sauce.

Make a bouquet garni by tying the rosemary, sage, thyme, and bay leaf together with kitchen twine. Tie the cloves in a small piece of cheesecloth. Add both to the sauce. Cover the pan with a lid and let simmer over low heat for about 2 hours, stirring from time to time.

When the duck is almost falling off the bone, remove from the sauce. Set the pan aside. If you would prefer to incorporate the meat into the sauce rather than serving the whole pieces of duck, remove and discard the duck skin. Pull the meat off the bone, then shred it into bite-sized pieces. Set aside.

Remove and discard the bouquet garni and the cloves. If the sauce seems thin, reduce it at a slow boil to the desired consistency. If you removed the duck meat from the bones, add it to the pan. Adjust the seasoning if necessary.

When ready to serve: Bring a large pot of salted water to a rolling boil.

Warm the duck ragu over medium-low heat. If serving whole pieces of duck meat, rewarm them in a 350°F oven.

Add the gnocchi to the boiling water. When the gnocchi float to the surface, taste one to see if it is cooked through. If necessary, simmer briefly to finish cooking. Remove the gnocchi with a slotted spoon and transfer to the duck sauce. Gently fold into the sauce, and adjust the seasoning as necessary.

Spoon the gnocchi and ragu into warm bowls and top with the grated Parmigiano. If serving the whole pieces of duck, serve them on a platter.

ROASTED DUCK WITH POTATOES AND PANCETTA
L'Anatra Arrosto

❀ Serves 6

THIS RECIPE COMES OUT OF the tradition of the harvest feast. Under the old sharecropper system, the most important time of year was the wheat harvest and threshing, the *trebbiatura*. If you think of all the Italian food that depends on pasta and bread, you have an idea of the place of that grain in our culture. Small farmers, my family among them, could not afford a thresher, so a group of households would go in on one and the men would go from farm to farm, pitching in with the hard work. "We used to carry forty-kilo sacks of grain from the field to the storeroom," the old-timers have told me. This was no small effort when you consider that the typical farmhouse had the animals on the ground floor, the wine on the next, the living quarters up another flight of stairs, and the storeroom on top!

Because the *trebbiatura* took place in the hot month of July, the work would start at midnight and go until noon. The men would take a break in the fields at dawn, when the women brought coffee and cake. Then they would pause again for a little cold meat at eight in the morning and finally, they would quit at noon, which would be the occasion of a big lunch. There were endless courses of duck, goose, beef, rabbit, and pork. And, of course, wine enough to fuel an afternoon snooze.

When we were growing up, my sister and I had a little *trebbiatura* of our own, only we "harvested" corn. We loved freshly picked corn with our roasted duck. We didn't have a farm—but there were farms nearby. Sometimes when we were riding through the country, my dad would pull the car to the side of the road and Claudia and I would hop a fence and "borrow" a few ears of corn to throw on the grill and have with our duck.

1 duck, about 4½ pounds, liver reserved	8 tablespoons (4 ounces) unsalted butter
1 cup whole milk	½ pound pancetta, cut into ¼-inch dice
Kosher salt and freshly ground black pepper	1 medium onion, finely chopped
1 garlic head, cut in half to expose the cloves	1 garlic clove, thinly sliced
4 sprigs rosemary	2 tablespoons Cognac
1 pound fingerling potatoes, peeled and cut into ¼-inch dice	Six ½-inch-thick slices crusty country bread, such as ciabatta

Six hours before cooking, place the duck liver in a small bowl and add the milk. Cover and refrigerate.

Two hours before cooking, season the duck generously with salt and pepper, inside and out. Insert half the garlic head and 2 sprigs of the rosemary in the cavity. Set the duck on a plate, cover with a kitchen towel, and let rest on the counter for 2 hours.

Preheat the oven to 425°F.

Place the potatoes in a saucepan, cover with water, and add 2 tablespoons salt. Bring to a boil over medium heat and cook for about 10 minutes, or until the potatoes are tender but still firm. Remove from the heat and let them cool in the cooking water.

Melt 6 tablespoons of the butter in a large ovenproof sauté pan or a flame-proof roasting pan over medium-low heat. Add the duck and sear on all sides until golden brown. As it cooks, use a large spoon to baste the duck with the butter and fat in the pan to ensure even coloring of the skin. Transfer the duck to a rack set over a baking sheet.

Remove any burned fat or duck scraps from the pan and return it to medium heat. Add the pancetta and sauté until crisp and golden. Add the onions and sauté for about 8 minutes, or until they soften and begin to caramelize. Place the duck in the center of the pan. Drain the potatoes and scatter them over the onions and pancetta. Add the remaining 2 rosemary sprigs and garlic.

Continued

Transfer the pan to the oven and roast for 30 to 35 minutes. Remove the pan from the oven, and let the duck rest for 20 minutes.

Meanwhile, preheat the broiler. Drain the liver and pat dry. Cut into large dice, about ½ inch. Season with a pinch each of salt and pepper.

Melt the remaining 2 tablespoons butter in a small sauté pan over medium-high heat. Add the sliced garlic. When the garlic is translucent, add the liver. Cook, stirring occasionally, for about 2 minutes, or until the liver is golden brown and firm to the touch. Add the cognac and light it with a long match (or, if using a gas burner, you can carefully tilt the pan toward the flame to ignite it). Let the flame die down, then season to taste with salt and pepper. Set aside, covered to keep warm.

Toast the bread under the broiler, turning once.

Carve the duck and arrange in the center of a serving platter. Drain off any excess fat from the potatoes and onions, and arrange around the duck. Top the toasted bread with the sautéed liver, and serve immediately with the duck.

BRAISED GUINEA HEN
Faraona nel Coccio

COCCIO IS MARCHIGIANI for a special clay cooking pot, unglazed terra-cotta on top and shiny black on the bottom. The best pots have always been made in the pretty little hill town of Fratterosa, an hour's drive from Osimo. The coccio makes me think of Graziella Belardinelli, my godmother. Even though she's country bred, from Santo Stefano, she has always dressed just so. Her apartment was across the street from ours. Although her life on the farm was by then a distant memory, she could be counted on to throw big farm-style dinners. We would all sit down at a long table, just as they used to do in the country—but this one was in front of the garage door of her apartment building, rather than in her country garden. This dish of guinea hen with tomatoes cooked in a gastrique—caramelized sugar and vinegar—was one she often served.

If guinea hen is not available at your market, you can substitute chicken, preferably organic.

1 guinea hen or organic chicken, about 4 pounds	1 cup dry white wine, such as Verdicchio or Pinot Grigio
Kosher salt and freshly ground black pepper	2 cups Chicken Stock (page 214)
1 head garlic, split in half to expose the cloves	1¼ cups coarsely chopped onions
1 small bunch sage	1 tablespoon granulated sugar
1 small bunch rosemary	¼ cup white wine vinegar
¾ cup extra virgin olive oil	1 pound plum tomatoes, peeled, seeded, and cut into chunks
8 tablespoons (4 ounces) unsalted butter	8 medium basil leaves

Season the guinea hen generously with salt and pepper, inside and out. Place half of the garlic, half of the sage, and half of the rosemary in the cavity. Place on a plate, cover, and set aside at room temperature for 1 hour.

Continued

Preheat the oven to 400°F.

In a flameproof clay pot or a Dutch oven, heat the olive oil over medium heat. Add the hen to the pot and sear on all sides until golden brown. Add 7 tablespoons of the butter, the remaining sage and rosemary, and the remaining garlic, cut side up, to the pot. Cook, using a large kitchen spoon to baste the guinea hen frequently, for about 10 minutes, adjusting the heat as necessary so that the butter doesn't burn.

Transfer the bird to a plate. Remove and discard the herbs and the garlic from the pot, and drain the fat.

Return the guinea hen to the pot and place over medium heat. Add the wine and simmer for 8 to 10 minutes, or until the wine is reduced by two-thirds. Add the chicken stock and bring to a simmer. Cover the pot and place in the oven for 20 minutes.

Meanwhile, bring a small saucepan of salted water to a rolling boil. Add the onions and blanch for 3 minutes; drain and set aside (blanching the onions before caramelizing them makes their flavor milder).

Melt the remaining 1 tablespoon butter in a large sauté pan over medium-high heat. Add the sugar and onions. Cook, stirring constantly, for about 4 to 6 minutes, until the sugar is completely dissolved and the onions are a deep caramel color.

Add the vinegar to the sauté pan and use a wooden spatula or spoon to scrape up any glaze clinging to the bottom of the pan. Add the tomatoes and sauté gently for about 5 minutes, until they are softened and glazed. Season to taste with salt and pepper. Tear the basil leaves in half and stir into the tomatoes. Remove from the heat and cover to keep warm.

To serve, transfer the tomatoes to a serving dish.

Bring the pot with the hen to the dining room and remove the lid at the table so everyone can enjoy the aroma. Carve the hen and serve accompanied by the tomatoes.

SPIT-ROASTED SQUAB

Piccioni allo Spiedo

❈ *Serves 6*

IN THE SAME WAY that a Cornish game hen is like a miniature chicken, a squab, or pigeon, is like rich wild game in a small package. The dark meat is so succulent that it is one of the few birds—wild or domestic—that doesn't dry out quickly when grilled over hot coals. In Italy, there is a saying "*En agosto, palombo rosto,*" which translates as "In August, roast pigeon." Actually, I like my squab to fatten up some more, as they will by the fall.

Before grilling, season the squab with crushed juniper berries, sage, garlic, and prosciutto, then baste with olive oil infused with herbs and citrus zest. This herb oil would also be great on grilled meats such as lamb or steaks.

If you don't have a grill with a spit, don't worry: The squab can also be roasted in a hot oven. This dish is even more splendid when washed down with a glass of brawny Le Marche Rosso Conero.

2 tablespoons crushed juniper berries	1 tablespoon chopped rosemary
Kosher salt and freshly ground black pepper	1 tablespoon chopped thyme
6 squab, about 1 pound each	3 bay leaves, preferably fresh, chopped
¾ cup extra virgin olive oil, plus more for brushing the birds	A ½-inch-wide strip of orange zest
18 sage leaves	A ½-inch-wide strip of lemon zest
9 garlic cloves, skin left on, crushed	½ cup dry white wine, such as Verdicchio or Pinot Grigio
⅔ pound thinly sliced prosciutto, cut into ⅛-inch-wide strips	

In a small bowl, combine the juniper berries, ¼ cup salt, and 1½ teaspoons pepper.

Wipe the inside of the birds dry with paper towels. Brush or rub the squab with olive oil, including the cavities. Season the birds inside and out with

Continued

the juniper mixture. Place the squab on a baking sheet. Stuff the cavity of each bird with 3 sage leaves, a garlic clove, and one-sixth of the prosciutto. Cover and let marinate at room temperature for 20 minutes.

Prepare a charcoal fire or gas grill with a spit, or preheat the oven to 400°F.

Place the ¾ cup olive oil in a medium saucepan and heat over medium heat just until warm. Remove from the heat, add the rosemary, thyme, bay leaves, orange and lemon zest, wine, and the remaining 3 garlic cloves, and mix well. Season to taste with salt and pepper. Set aside.

If using a grill fitted with a spit, skewer the squab on the spit. Cook for about 20 minutes, using a pastry brush to baste the birds with the herb oil every 5 minutes. Or place the squab in a large roasting pan and roast in the oven for about 20 minutes, basting every 5 minutes with the oil. When the squab is done, its skin will be crispy and golden and the breast meat will be medium to medium-rare. Transfer to a platter, cover loosely, and let rest in a warm place for 10 minutes before serving.

ROASTED TURKEY BREAST STUFFED WITH OLIVES AND HERBS

Tacchino alla Picena

❋ Serves 6

TURKEY IS, of course, not originally from Le Marche—but then neither are tomatoes, nor, for that matter, pasta. But we have taken these imports and made them very much our own. On its own, turkey cannot be said to be the most interesting meat, but this lack of flash becomes a virtue when you prepare a turkey breast as they do in Piceno with fragrant herbs, pancetta, and olives.

Caul fat is available in ethnic markets and from specialty butchers. I am all in favor of more people using this original, natural, and entirely edible wrapper. (Note that it needs to be soaked in lemon water overnight before using.)

½ pound caul fat, in one piece

1 lemon, halved

¼ cup finely chopped dill fronds, stems reserved

¼ cup finely chopped basil leaves, stems reserved

¼ cup finely chopped Italian parsley leaves, stems reserved

¼ cup finely chopped marjoram leaves, stems reserved

3 chicken livers, cleaned and cut into ¼-inch dice

3 tablespoons extra virgin olive oil

¾ pound Ascolana olives or other flavorful olives, pitted and chopped

Kosher salt and freshly ground black pepper

4 cups dry white wine, such as Verdicchio or Pinot Grigio

1 boneless, skinless turkey breast, about 2½ pounds

⅓ pound thinly sliced pancetta

¼ pound manteca (soft lard; see Sources, page 223)

To clean the caul fat, place it in a bowl of cold water with the juice of half the lemon. Set aside to soak for several hours, swishing the fat in the water from time to time to remove the blood. Change the water and add the juice from the remaining lemon half. Soak overnight in the refrigerator.

Continued

Early the next day, stuff the turkey breast: In a large bowl, combine the chopped herbs, chicken livers, olive oil, and olives. Season lightly with salt and pepper. Sauté a small patty of the stuffing in a small skillet. Taste for seasoning, and reseason as necessary. Cover and refrigerate.

Using your hands, tear the reserved herb stems into pieces and toss them into a large saucepan. Add the wine and bring to a simmer over medium-high heat. Simmer for about 15 minutes, or until the wine reduces by half. Remove the saucepan from the heat and let cool to room temperature.

Use a sharp knife to cut a pocket in the turkey breast: Make an incision along one long side of the breast, starting 1 inch from the thickest end and continuing until you are 1 inch from the other end of the breast; work the knife back and forth until you have a deep pocket in the meat. Fill the pocket with the stuffing. Place the breast in a resealable plastic bag. Pour the herb-infused wine into the bag and seal, squeezing out the excess air. Refrigerate for 8 hours, turning the bag over after 4 hours.

Cut half a dozen or so pieces of kitchen twine long enough to encircle the turkey breast.

Remove the caul fat from the water and dry thoroughly with paper towels. Spread fat on a clean work surface. Starting in the center of the caul fat and working outward, arrange the pieces of pancetta in a rough rectangle the same size as the turkey breast. Remove the turkey breast from the marinade (reserve the marinade), pat dry with paper towels, and season lightly with salt and pepper. Place the breast skinned side down on the pancetta. Roll the breast up in the caul fat, trimming away any excess; secure it with the twine, tying it at 1-inch intervals, without squeezing or compressing the meat. Let stand at room temperature for 20 minutes.

Preheat the oven to 450°F.

Grease a medium roasting pan with a thin coating of the manteca. Place the turkey breast in the pan and roast for 20 minutes, basting frequently with the reserved marinade. Turn the turkey breast over, and reduce the heat to 400°F. Cook for an additional 20 minutes, basting frequently. To test if the turkey is done, stick a fork in the thickest part of the breast: the juices should run clear.

Remove from the oven, cover with aluminum foil, and let rest on the stovetop for 25 minutes.

Cut the twine from the meat, and slice into thick pieces. Skim the fat from the roasting juices, and serve the juices with the turkey.

Meat

ROASTED VEAL CHOPS WITH HONEY
Cotoletta di Vitello al Miele

❀ *Serves 6*

WE ALWAYS BOUGHT OUR VEAL—delicate in texture but deep and rich in taste—from Nello Salvucci, our favorite butcher. Like so many of our friends, he was another transplant from the farm in Santo Stefano. I loved going to see him after the Thursday market in town, and as I grew older, I used to hang around his shop asking questions about meat. Nello gave me a big education; all about butchering, deboning, and the ins and outs of meat.

The sauce for this veal dish is made with grapes and honey (in the old days, families like ours would have used honey as a sweetener instead of the more costly cane sugar). One of my favorites is corbezzolo honey, made from the nectar of the arbutus shrub—also called strawberry tree—whose flowers can be seen all over the countryside of Le Marche and Piemonte. In addition to the sweetness, it has a bitter note that works almost as a palate refresher.

6 veal rib chops, about 8 ounces each and 1 inch thick	2 bay leaves, preferably fresh
Kosher salt and freshly ground black pepper	2 sprigs sage
¾ pound seedless green grapes	4 oil-packed anchovy fillets, chopped
4 tablespoons (2 ounces) unsalted butter, plus 4 tablespoons (2 ounces) cold unsalted butter	2 cups dry white wine, such as Verdicchio or Pinot Grigio
8 whole cloves	1½ cups Chicken Stock (page 214)
	2 tablespoons Corbezzolo honey (see Sources, page 223) or other aromatic honey

Season the veal chops lightly with salt and pepper. Place on a plate, cover, and let rest for 30 minutes.

Slice the grapes lengthwise in half. Set aside.

Place two large sauté pans over medium-high heat. Melt 2 tablespoons of the butter in each pan. Add 3 chops to each pan and brown them for about 3 minutes on each side. Add half of the cloves, bay leaves, sage, and anchovies to each pan. Sauté for 3 minutes.

Add 1 cup of wine to each pan and bring to a boil, scraping the browned bits from the bottom with a wooden spatula or spoon. Cook until the wine has almost completely evaporated.

Turn the chops and add ¾ cup of the chicken stock to each pan. Bring to a simmer and cook the veal for 4 minutes. Turn the veal over and simmer for an additional 4 minutes, or until cooked to medium. Transfer the veal to a serving dish and cover with aluminum foil to keep warm.

Pour the cooking liquid from both pans through a fine-mesh strainer into a saucepan. Bring to a boil, then reduce the heat and simmer for 5 minutes. Add the grapes and honey, stir, and cook for 4 minutes.

Stir the remaining 4 tablespoons cold butter bit by bit into the sauce. Season to taste with salt and pepper. Spoon the sauce over the veal chops and serve.

BEEF TENDERLOIN WITH FONDUE OF TALAMELLO CHEESE
Filetto all'Ambra di Talamello

❀ *Serves 6*

RECENTLY *FOOD & WINE* MAGAZINE asked me for some recipes inspired by Le Marche. Because America is a beef-loving country, I thought I'd dream up something I could make with our amazing beef cattle called razza marchigiana (they are related to the giant Tuscan Chianina—and, in my opinion, better). Then I thought of the Philadelphia cheese steak, which surprised me the first time I had it: I was expecting a sirloin with cheese on it. This, then, is my marchigiani homage to the cheese steak—hopefully a bit more refined than the original.

6 beef tenderloin steaks, about 8 ounces each and ¾ inch thick

Kosher salt and freshly ground white pepper

5 tablespoons extra virgin olive oil

6 slices Ambra di Talamello cheese or Italian Fontina or Taleggio, about 3 inches × 3 inches and ⅛ inch thick

2 ounces black truffles, shaved or thinly sliced (optional)

Prepare a charcoal fire or preheat a gas grill. Or preheat a cast-iron grill pan over high heat.

Twenty to 30 minutes before grilling, remove the beef from the refrigerator and season lightly with salt and pepper. Put on a plate, cover, and set aside.

Just before grilling, brush each steak generously with olive oil. Grill the beef over medium-high heat for 3 to 4 minutes per side, for medium-rare. One minute before the tenderloins are done, place a slice of cheese on each and cover the grill or pan to allow the cheese to soften (just like on a cheeseburger). Transfer to a plate and let rest in a warm spot for 5 minutes.

Top each steak with slices of truffle, if using, and serve.

BAKED STUFFED ZUCCHINI
Zucchini in Umido

AS ANYONE WHO GARDENS knows, when zucchini comes into season, if you have one ripe zucchini, you probably have a hundred more: this vegetable arrives en masse. This was always seen as an opportunity by my Nonna Palmina. Every possible combination of zucchini that she tried always came out perfect. Her cardinal principle—"Never waste any ingredient or leftover"—guided her through endless variations of this recipe. Often the talk around her dinner table turned to how the townspeople had to hide their food during the Second World War; otherwise the soldiers would have come and cleaned out the larder. This zucchini in umido, though, is for peaceful and prosperous times.

6 medium zucchini, about 6 inches long and 1¼ inches in diameter

Kosher salt and freshly ground black pepper

¼ cup plus 2 tablespoons extra virgin olive oil

1 medium onion, finely chopped

2¾ cups peeled, seeded, and diced (¼-inch) plum tomatoes (about 2 pounds tomatoes)

7 tablespoons (3½ ounces) unsalted butter

¼ pound pancetta, cut into ¼-inch dice

¾ pound veal loin, cut into ¼-inch dice

¼ pound white mushrooms, trimmed and cut into ¼-inch dice

1 cup freshly grated Parmigiano-Reggiano (about 4 ounces)

1 tablespoon grated lemon zest

3 large egg yolks, lightly beaten

2 tablespoons finely chopped Italian parsley

Bring a large pot of salted water to a rolling boil. Cut off the ends of the zucchini and slice the zucchini into 2-inch lengths. Remove the center of each section with an apple corer, melon baller, or small paring knife to form a tube, leaving a shell about ¼ inch thick.

Continued

Prepare a large bowl of ice water. Blanch the zucchini in the boiling water for 1 minute, then plunge into the ice water. Drain and pat dry. Place the zucchini on a plate, season with salt and pepper, and drizzle with 2 tablespoons of the olive oil.

Preheat the oven to 375°F.

Heat the remaining ¼ cup olive oil in a large saucepan over medium-high heat. Add the onion and cook for about 4 minutes, or until soft and translucent, stirring occasionally. Add the tomatoes and cook for 8 to 10 minutes, until they soften and break down. Season to taste with salt and pepper. Spread the mixture evenly in a 9-by-13-inch baking dish.

Melt 3 tablespoons of the butter in a sauté pan large enough to hold the diced pancetta and veal in a single layer over medium heat. (If your pan is not large enough, sear the meat in two batches.) Increase the heat to medium-high and add the pancetta. As soon it starts to brown, add the veal and sauté for 6 to 8 minutes, or until golden brown. Drain the pancetta and veal mixture in a colander to remove excess fat, then transfer to a large bowl.

Return the pan to the burner and reduce the heat to medium. Add the remaining 4 tablespoons butter. Once it melts, add the mushrooms and sauté for about 5 minutes, or until golden. Drain and add them to the meat.

Add the Parmigiano, lemon zest, and yolks to the meat mixture and mix well. Season the stuffing with salt and pepper. Form a small patty of the meat and sauté it in a small skillet to check the seasoning. Reseason as needed.

Fill each zucchini tube with the stuffing and use your hands to smooth the ends. Stand the tubes upright in the baking dish. At this point the dish can be covered and refrigerated for up to a day (the baking time will be somewhat longer). Cover with aluminum foil and bake for about 12 minutes, or until heated through.

Sprinkle the zucchini with the parsley and serve immediately.

ABOVE: CHICKEN WITH ROSEMARY, GARLIC, AND TOMATO SAUCE *(Pollo in Potacchio)*, PAGE 128.
TOP LEFT: ROASTED VEAL CHOPS WITH HONEY *(Cotoletta di Vitello al Miele)*, PAGE 196. BOTTOM
LEFT: LE MARCHE-STYLE BOLLITO MISTO *(Il Lesso)*, PAGE 15.

Slow-Braised Meat and Vegetables (*Umido*), page 154.

Roasted Suckling Pig Ascolana-Style (*Porchetta Ascolana*), page 166.

Crispy Fried Pastry Cream Squares (*Crema Fritta*), page 178.

CHILDREN'S CRESCIA *(Crescia dei Bambini)*, PAGE 186.

SWEET ORANGE AND RAISIN BREAD (*Ciambella*), PAGE 203.

LE MARCHE-STYLE BOLLITO MISTO
Il Lesso

THIS IS ONE OF THE MANY—sometimes seemingly endless—courses served at Le Marche weddings. Although we think of the food part of the festivities as "lunch," it is a six-hour feast. As with the traditional bollito misto served in nearby Umbria, we first serve the broth (the braising liquid) on its own. Then we serve the meat and vegetables. You might think that after these two courses you would feel well satisfied, but that is just the beginning. There will typically also be a fritto misto, some stuffed olives, vincisgrassi, tagliatelle, umido (see page 154), and on and on.

The meats used for the bollito can be adjusted according to your preference or what is available from your butcher. This recipe is for the classic dish, a feast in itself, but you could choose just two or three meats. I do recommend including poultry, beef, and veal, and at least one bone, since bones add flavor and body to the broth. If you do not have a stockpot large enough (you will need a very big one) to hold all the ingredients, make it in two pots, or cut the recipe in half. Use any leftover broth to cook pasta.

1 organic chicken, 4 to 5 pounds	6 whole cloves
1 duck, 6 to 8 pounds	Kosher salt
3 pig's feet	1 tablespoon crushed black peppercorns
¾ pound oxtails—6 to 8 pieces, about ½ inch thick	1 celery heart, cut into chunks
6 center-cut beef marrow bones, each about 3 inches long	3 carrots, cut into chunks
1 beef eye of round, about 3 pounds	3 medium onions, skin left on, cut in half
1 veal or beef knuckle	1 bay leaf, preferably fresh
1 veal breast, about 3 pounds	1 sprig rosemary
A large piece of Parmigiano-Reggiano rind	1 sprig thyme

Continued

¼ cup Italian parsley sprigs

1 sage leaf

Freshly ground black pepper

Vegetables, such as green beans, carrots, and celery, all cut into the size of a green bean (optional)

Fleur de sel

Salsa Verde (page 96)

Extra virgin olive oil for drizzling

Pat dry the chicken and duck, inside and out, with paper towels. Remove all organs from the cavity of the chicken and the duck. This is important because they can emit a bitter taste when braised for a long period of time.

Bring a large pot of water to a rolling boil. Add the pig's feet and blanch for 3 minutes. Drain and rinse under cold water.

Place the chicken, duck, pig's feet, oxtails, marrow bones, top round, veal knuckle, veal breast, Parmigiano rind, cloves, ¼ cup kosher salt, and crushed peppercorns in a very large pot. Cover the meats with cold water by about 1 inch and bring to a simmer over medium-high heat. Skim off the impurities and fat that have risen to the surface. Add the celery, carrots, and onions, reduce the heat, and simmer gently for 1½ hours; continue to skim frequently throughout the cooking.

Remove the chicken and duck. Place on a large tray and check to see if they are fully cooked by piercing the thickest part of a thigh with a sharp knife; the juices should be clear and the meat should no longer be pink. Return briefly to the pot if necessary. Once the chicken and duck are fully cooked, transfer to a large baking dish or other shallow container and spoon a little of the cooking liquid over them. Refrigerate, loosely covered.

Simmer for another hour or so, or until the veal breast is fork-tender. Transfer it to the dish with the poultry and re-cover.

Simmer for another hour. Transfer the top round and pig's feet to a tray. Cover loosely with plastic wrap.

Simmer for another 2 hours (5½ hours total cooking time). Transfer the oxtails to a tray and cover loosely.

Strain the broth into another stockpot. The celery, carrots, and onion will have lost most of their flavor, but they can be served with the meats, if desired.

Tie the bay leaf, rosemary, thyme, parsley, and sage together and add to the stockpot. Bring to a fast simmer and cook for about 1 hour, or until the broth is reduced by half.

Cut the chicken and the duck into 8 pieces each (2 legs, 2 thighs, and 4 pieces breast). Cut the veal breast and top round into 6 thick slices each. In Le Marche, we let each diner remove the skin from the pig's feet; or you can do it, and discard the bone. Add all the meats to the stockpot and simmer gently just until heated through. Transfer all of the meats to a large serving bowl.

Strain the broth once more through a fine-mesh strainer into a clean pot. Bring to a boil, then reduce to a simmer and check the seasoning, adding salt and pepper as necessary. If adding vegetables to the dish, simmer them in the stock until tender. Using a slotted spoon, transfer them to the bowl of meats.

Ladle the broth over the meats and sprinkle with kosher salt. Serve the bollito misto in soup bowls, accompanied by fleur de sel, salsa verde, and a cruet of olive oil for drizzling.

SLOW-BRAISED MEATS AND VEGETABLES
Umido

❀ Serves 6

THIS LONG-COOKED BRAISE of meats, vegetables, and wine is just about the heartiest meal I know. When I was growing up, it was one of our Sunday meals. My father would start it early in the morning when the rest of us were still asleep, and at some point the aroma of the simmering meats served as my wake-up call. I would make my way into the kitchen, rub the sleep from my eyes, and sip at the mocha cappuccino that I drank every Sunday. Meanwhile, the mouthwatering smell of the umido grew stronger and stronger.

Miraculously, guests at Italian wedding parties manage to find room for this dish alongside il lesso (see page 151). Perhaps all the dancing works up their appetite. Traditionally umido is made with veal, oxtail, chicken, spareribs, prosciutto, cotechino sausage, and pork belly, each meat adding another layer of flavor and texture. While it is not absolutely necessary to use the lard and pork belly, these ingredients give the stew extra depth. Just make sure you use high-quality pork, free range if possible.

1 piece veal shank (osso buco), about 1¼ pounds

2 pieces oxtail, about 8 ounces each

1 chicken leg

1 chicken breast

1 slab pork spareribs (2 to 3 pounds), cut into 2 pieces

1½ pounds pork belly (optional)

1 cotechino (see Note) or other Italian pork sausage, about 1½ pounds

Kosher salt and freshly ground black pepper

5 ounces manteca (soft lard; see Sources, page 223)

¼ pound prosciutto, cut into ¼-inch dice

1 onion, finely diced

1 carrot, finely diced

1 celery stalk, finely diced

3 garlic cloves, chopped

1 bottle (750 ml) dry red wine, such as Montepulciano or Zinfandel

One 14.5-ounce can plum tomatoes, drained

1 sprig sage

1 sprig rosemary

1 sprig thyme

3 bay leaves, preferably fresh

4 cups Chicken Stock (page 214)

Generously season all the meats, including the pork belly, if using, with salt and pepper. Place a large Dutch oven or other heavy pot over medium-high heat, add half the lard, and heat until hot. Add the meats, in batches, and sear until golden brown on all sides. Transfer the meats to a platter and set aside in a warm spot.

Preheat the oven to 350°F.

Drain the fat from the pot and return it to medium heat. Add the remaining lard and heat until hot, then add the prosciutto. Cook for about 1 minute, or until golden. Add the onion, carrot, celery, and garlic and cook for about 10 minutes, or until very soft. Add the wine and use a wooden spatula or spoon to scrape all of the browned bits from the bottom of the pot. Bring the wine to a slow boil and cook for about 15 minutes, or until it has reduced by about two-thirds.

Add the tomatoes, crushing them with your hands, and their liquid to the sauce. Reduce the heat and simmer for 5 minutes.

Arrange the meats in the pot, or transfer the sauce to a large flameproof terra-cotta baking dish and add the meats. Tie the sage, rosemary, and thyme together with kitchen twine and submerge in the sauce. Stir in the bay leaves and chicken stock.

Bring to a simmer, then cover the pot and place in the oven. The meats will cook in different amounts of time; as you remove them, place them in a large baking dish and keep covered with aluminum foil at room temperature. Remove the chicken breast after 30 minutes, the chicken leg after 45 minutes, the cotechino after 1 hour, the spareribs and osso bucco after 2 hours, and the oxtail and pork belly, if using, after 3 hours of cooking.

Continued

Return the pot of braising liquid to the stove (leave the oven on) and bring the sauce to a slow boil over medium-high heat. Cook until reduced by one-third; the sauce should be thick, like a chowder. Season to taste with salt and pepper.

Spoon the sauce over the braised meats. Cover and place in the oven for 20 minutes, or until the meats are hot and the sauce is at a slow simmer. Serve.

NOTE Cotechino is a pork sausage from Modena. It is available at gourmet and Italian specialty stores; see Sources, page 223.

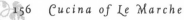

MY FATHER'S GRILLED PORK CHOPS
Giuseppe's Braciole

❖ Serves 6

ONE OF MY favorite recipes, this is also one of my father's favorites. One reason is, of course, that it is delicious, but the other may be that back when he was living on the farm, the prime cuts of pork usually went to the countess who owned the land. My father's family were left with the so-called lesser cuts, such as pig's brains, which were said to be good for kids. When the chance came to cook some prime cuts, my dad, the grillmaster in the family, was happy to show his stuff. I am willing to bet you could go back through all the generations of Trabocchis and you will find them equally skilled at and in love with this classic charcoal-grilled marinated pork chop. The herbs and citrus rind in the marinade are a perfect foil to the powerful meat flavor. You could use this same marinade on lamb chops.

In order to allow the flavor of the pork chops to fully develop, it is important to marinate the meat overnight. The chops are best grilled over charcoal and soaked wood chips.

6 pork chops, 8 to 12 ounces each,
    preferably organic
Kosher salt and freshly ground black pepper
1 orange
Grated zest of 1 lemon
3 garlic cloves, skin left on, crushed

Five 4-inch sprigs rosemary,
    leaves removed and finely
    chopped
3 whole cloves
¼ cup plus 2 tablespoons extra
    virgin olive oil

Wipe the pork chops dry and lightly season with salt and pepper. Grate the zest of the orange into a small bowl. Add the lemon zest, garlic, rosemary, cloves, and olive oil. Mix well.

Put the pork chops in a baking dish and pour the marinade over them. Turn to coat, rubbing the marinade into the meat. Squeeze the juice of the

Continued

Meat   157

orange over the chops, turn again, and cover tightly. (You can also marinate the chops in a resealable plastic bag.) Refrigerate overnight.

Remove the pork chops from the marinade and pat dry with paper towels. Discard the marinade. Place on a plate and let stand at room temperature for 30 minutes.

Meanwhile, prepare a charcoal fire or preheat a gas grill. Or preheat a cast-iron grill pan over medium-high heat.

Grill the pork chops for about 4 minutes per side, or until medium to medium-rare (they will continue to cook as they rest). Transfer the chops to a tray and let them rest for 10 minutes in a warm place before serving.

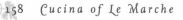

BRAISED SPARERIBS WITH POLENTA
Frescarelli con le Costarelle

❉ *Serves 6*

ALTHOUGH POLENTA is nothing more than lovingly prepared cornmeal mush, Marchigiani are extremely particular that it be exactly the right cornmeal and precisely the right water. In fact, in the village of Corinaldo, where I cooked for a number of years, the inhabitants will use only the water from one particular well for their polenta. As the story goes, a miller fell into that well over a thousand years ago and, through some miraculous transformation, the sacks of flour that went down with him still give a special taste to the well water and, in turn, Corinaldo polenta. Nice, but the only problem is, they didn't have corn in Italy until after the discovery of the New World five hundred years ago!

At any rate, the sauces that go with polenta are endless and, like most things in the cuisine of the common people, it is usually a matter of what's on hand. This sparerib stew was a favorite accompaniment in my home, where polenta was always served poured onto a thick wooden board that our friend Marcello, the carpenter, had cut for us. Although you can use white polenta flour here, traditionally frescarelli has always been made with fine Italian wheat flour. The result is a pleasantly lumpy porridge with a smooth texture, unlike the graininess that remains even in long-cooked cornmeal polenta.

Spareribs

2 slabs pork spareribs (about 3 pounds each)

Kosher salt and freshly ground black pepper

⅓ cup sunflower or peanut oil

6 mild Italian sausages

2 medium onions, thinly sliced

4 garlic cloves, thinly sliced

1 tablespoon tomato paste

2 cups dry white wine, such as Verdicchio or Pinot Grigio

4 whole cloves

2¼ cups drained and crushed canned Italian plum tomatoes

5 cups Chicken Stock (page 214)

5 sprigs rosemary

Continued

Frescarelli

9 cups water

Kosher salt

5 sprigs rosemary

1 garlic clove

2 ⅔ cups Italian 00 flour or white polenta
  flour (see Sources, page 223)

8 tablespoons (4 ounces) unsalted butter,
  softened

Freshly ground black pepper

¾ cup grated mild pecorino

Extra virgin olive oil for drizzling

FOR THE SPARERIBS

Slice the racks into individual ribs. Season generously with salt and pepper.

Pour the sunflower oil into a large roasting pan. Working in batches over medium-high heat, sear the ribs on both sides until golden brown. Transfer to a plate and set aside. Sear the sausages to brown on all sides. Set aside. Drain the excess fat from the pan.

Add the onions and garlic to the pan and sauté over medium-high heat for about 8 minutes, or until the onions begin to brown and caramelize. Add the tomato paste and stir for 1 minute. Return the ribs and sausages to the pan and add the wine. Bring to a boil over high heat, using a wooden spatula or spoon to scrape all of the browned bits from the bottom of the pan. Cook for 10 to 15 minutes, or until the wine has almost completely evaporated.

Tie the cloves in a piece of cheesecloth. Add to the pan, along with the tomatoes, chicken stock, and rosemary. Reduce the heat and bring the sauce just to a simmer. Cover and simmer gently for 45 minutes.

WHILE THE RIBS ARE COOKING, START THE FRESCARELLI

In a large saucepan, combine the water, 1 tablespoon salt, rosemary, and garlic. Bring to a boil, then reduce to a simmer and, using a slotted spoon, remove and discard the rosemary and garlic. Gradually add the flour (or polenta) in a thin stream, whisking constantly. Once it is fully incorporated, whisk for 1 minute. Reduce the heat to low and cook for 45 minutes, stirring vigorously every 5 to 10 minutes, until the frescarelli begins to thicken.

Meanwhile, after the ribs and sausages have cooked for 45 minutes, uncover, raise the heat slightly to keep the sauce at a simmer, and cook for 20 minutes longer. Season with salt and pepper and keep warm.

When the frescarelli is cooked, remove it from the heat and let stand for 5 minutes. Fold in the butter and season to taste with salt and pepper. Cover to keep warm and set aside.

Spoon the frescarelli onto a large serving platter. Top with the ribs, sausages, and sauce. Sprinkle the pecorino over the top and drizzle with olive oil.

WHITE BEANS WITH SALT PORK
Fagioli con le Cotiche

PERHAPS NOTHING is more typical of farmhouse food life than these long-cooked beans served on a cold winter's day. I remember a trip we made one winter up to Mt. Vettore in Ascoli Piceno. I was chilled to the bone. We pulled over to a little taverna where they had just finished serving lunch, but there were still some baked beans left. They were so warm and filling, I was as happy as if I had come upon a feast. My father recalled how, after a hard day of work on the family farm, he'd often come home to a copper pot of beans and salt pork that had been simmering for hours. After such a meal, he assured us, cold weather was no longer an issue.

2 cups dried cannellini beans, picked over and rinsed	2 garlic cloves, thinly sliced
1 teaspoon baking powder	¼ pound prosciutto, cut into ¼-inch dice
½ pound salt pork or pancetta	3 tablespoons finely chopped Italian parsley
1 sprig rosemary	4 canned plum tomatoes, drained, seeded, and finely chopped
½ cup extra virgin olive oil, plus more for drizzling	Six ½-inch-thick slices crusty country bread, such as ciabatta, toasted
1 medium onion, thinly sliced	Freshly ground black pepper

Place the beans and baking soda in a large bowl. (The baking soda will help soften the beans.) Add enough cold water to cover by 2 inches, and let soak overnight at room temperature.

To prepare the salt pork, bring a large saucepan of water to a rolling boil. Use a knife to remove the rind from the salt pork. Blanch the salt pork in the boiling water for 10 minutes. Drain and let cool.

Cut the salt pork or pancetta into ½-inch cubes and put in a medium saucepan. Add enough cold water to cover by ½ inch. Bring the water to a simmer. Add the rosemary and cook for about 30 minutes if using salt pork, or until tender, adding more water as necessary to keep it covered by ¼ inch; or simmer the pancetta for 10 minutes. Remove from the heat and set aside.

Meanwhile, drain the beans and place in a medium saucepan. Add enough fresh cold water to cover by 2 inches. Bring to a simmer over medium-high heat and cook the beans at a gentle simmer for about 35 minutes, or until tender. Use a ladle to skim any impurities from the surface of the cooking liquid as necessary. Remove from the heat and set aside.

Heat the oil in a large saucepan over medium-high heat. Add the onion, garlic, prosciutto, and parsley and sauté until the onion and garlic are lightly golden, about 8 minutes, stirring occasionally. Add the tomatoes and sauté until softened, about 5 minutes. Drain the salt pork or pancetta and add to the pan, along with the beans and their cooking liquid. Bring to a simmer, skimming the surface as necessary. Partially cover the saucepan, reduce the heat, and gently simmer for 20 minutes, or until the beans are very tender and the salt pork is translucent.

Serve in bowls, with the toasted bread. Top each bowl with a drizzle of olive oil and some pepper.

GRILLED PORK LIVER WITH BAY LEAF
Fegatelli alla Brace

❋ *Serves 6*

WHEN AN AMERICAN thinks of meat on the grill, it is usually something like a burger or steak or ribs. A Marchigiano is just as likely to picture pig's liver—which I have never seen on a menu in the United States. That's a shame, because it is so satisfying and flavorful. We usually have it as part of a mixed grill. I remember when I was about twelve, we drove up in the mountains to Amandola on a cold day in late autumn. We stopped for hot chocolate at a tavern that was full of families like our own, as well as a lot of hunters. At a huge hearth, a plump fellow tended meat on the fire. He worked with an array of game birds, venison, beef steaks, and pig's liver wrapped in aromatic bay laurel leaves.

Although you could make a version of this dish with large, plump chicken livers, I urge you to try it with pork liver. You can find pork liver at Asian or Latino markets; be sure it is very fresh (or you will not appreciate its flavor). Caul fat is available in ethnic markets and at specialty butchers; note that it must be soaked overnight.

Serve the pork livers with white beans (page 162) or a salad and grilled country bread.

⅔ pound caul fat

1 lemon, halved

1¾ pounds pork liver (about half of one liver)

Kosher salt and freshly ground black pepper

1½ cups dry bread crumbs

1 cup freshly grated Parmigiano-Reggiano

6 bay leaves, preferably fresh, cut or broken in half

Six ½-inch-thick slices crusty country bread, such as ciabatta

Lemon wedges for serving

To clean the caul fat, soak the fat in cold water with the juice of half the lemon for several hours at room temperature, swishing the fat in the water from time to time to remove any blood. Change the water, and add the juice from the other lemon half. Soak overnight in the refrigerator.

Soak about 24 bamboo skewers in cold water.

Drain the caul fat and place on paper towels. Pat dry. Divide the caul fat into 12 pieces, large enough to wrap around the individual pieces of liver.

Cut the pork liver into 12 strips about ½ inch thick. Season the strips lightly with salt and pepper on both sides. Combine the bread crumbs and Parmigiano in a large bowl.

Place the caul fat on a clean work surface and lay half a bay leaf on top of each piece.

Dip a strip of liver in the bread crumb mixture, coating both sides. Place in the center of a piece of caul fat and wrap in the fat. Insert 2 bamboo skewers lengthwise through the liver to help it hold its shape when grilled. Place on a plate. Repeat with the remaining strips. Refrigerate for 20 minutes.

Prepare a charcoal fire, or preheat the gas grill. Or preheat a cast-iron grill pan over high heat.

Place the livers on the grill (or in the grill pan) and cook for about 3 minutes per side for pork liver, 2 minutes per side for chicken liver, or until the caul fat dissolves and the liver begins to crisp. Serve immediately, with lemon wedges.

Roasted Suckling Pig Ascolana-Style

Porchetta Ascolana

❊ *Serves 8*

THIS PORCHETTA is one of the great prides of Le Marche gastronomy. Whole roast pig is found all over Italy, but Marchigiani say theirs is the original. The people of Ascoli Piceno go one step further and say the rest of Le Marche learned from them. Yet when I stopped to consider those claims, I thought, "How silly!" The technique of roasting a whole pig surely occurred many times in many places. All that is required is a pig and a fire.

To enjoy porchetta in Le Marche, you don't necessarily have to make it at home. On market day (Thursday in Osimo), people buy porchetta sandwiches the way Americans buy hot dogs at a football game. It is also a tradition to prepare this as a feast every year on August 15, Ferragosto (Assumption Day), with the whole family involved in the project—beginning with choosing the right pig. My homage to this classic features suckling pig stuffed with the rich shoulder meat from a mature pig, a delicious contrast to its delicate flesh. My customers won't let me take it off the menu. Although the pig and its pork stuffing must marinate overnight, for such a special dish, this is surprisingly uncomplicated. And your guests will never forget it.

This is really a feast, and it needs no other accompaniment than a simple salad.

You will need to order the suckling pig from a specialty butcher; ask them to bone out the pig for you too.

---

1 small suckling pig, about 8 to 10 pounds, boned

4 cups dry white wine, such as Verdicchio or Pinot Grigio

3¼ pounds boneless pork butt or shoulder, cut into ½-inch dice

Kosher salt and freshly ground black pepper

3 bunches dill

8 to 10 garlic cloves, crushed

1¾ pounds manteca (soft lard; see Sources, page 223)

DAY 1

Lay the pig skin side down in a roasting pan or on a rimmed baking sheet. Pour the wine over the flesh and massage it into the meat. Season both the pig and the pork butt with salt and pepper. Scatter the pork butt over the inside of the pig, cover evenly with the dill sprigs, and scatter the garlic cloves over the top. Wrap the pan in plastic wrap and refrigerate overnight.

DAY 2

Remove the pig from the refrigerator. Remove the dill and garlic from the pig; set the garlic aside. Separate the dill fronds from the stems, and discard the stems. Combine the dill fronds, garlic, and half the lard in a food processor. Pulse 4 or 5 times to mix, then process to form a paste. Season lightly with salt and pepper and transfer to a bowl.

Remove the pork butt from the cavity and set aside. Using your hands, spread the dill paste evenly over the flesh of the pig. Distribute the pork butt evenly inside the cavity, from neck to tail. Fold the edges of the cavity over so the pig resembles a long roll. Cover with plastic wrap and refrigerate for 1 hour.

Preheat the oven to 375°F.

Using a kitchen needle and kitchen twine, sew up the cavity of the pig: Begin at the legs and work up to the head. Turn the pig over and, using your hands, shape the body into a uniform cylinder. Tie the body with kitchen twine at 1-inch intervals so the pig maintains its shape during cooking.

Place a rack in the roasting pan or on the baking sheet. Place the pig belly side down on the rack and roast for 25 minutes.

Meanwhile, melt the remaining manteca in a small saucepan. Keep warm.

Remove the pig from the oven and, using a pastry brush, baste with some of the melted manteca. Return the pig to the oven, increase the heat to 425°F, and roast for about 40 minutes longer, basting every 10 minutes with manteca. The pig is ready when the skin is crisp and golden and the internal temperature is at least 145°F. Remove the pig from the oven and let rest on the stovetop for 30 minutes.

To serve, carve into 1-inch-thick slices, removing the twine from each piece.

FRITTO MISTO OF LAMB, ZUCCHINI, AND ARTICHOKES
Fritto Misto all'Ascolana

❋ *Serves 6*

CHANCES ARE that if you know fritto misto, it is the familiar Tuscan version: a potpourri of fried fish, shellfish, and vegetables. But lamb is often served this way with fried zucchini in Ascoli. Just as veal can be pounded into thin scallops, so can lamb. I prefer rib chops with a nice big eye for this recipe. The traditional Ascoli version of this fritto misto also includes olives Ascolana (page 14) and crema fritta (page 178). Be advised, there is a lot of breading and frying involved, but I have never seen any leftovers from this meal. And it always does a cook's heart good to see his or her creation disappear in a hurry.

Juice of ½ lemon	4 large eggs
12 baby artichokes	2 cups Italian 00 flour or all-purpose flour
6 medium zucchini, rinsed well and patted dry	2 cups dry bread crumbs
12 rib lamb chops, about 1 inch thick	2½ quarts sunflower or peanut oil
Kosher salt and freshly ground black pepper	Lemon wedges for serving

FOR THE ARTICHOKES

Combine the lemon juice with 4 cups water in a large bowl. Working with 1 artichoke at a time, cut off ¼ inch from the top and discard. Trim the bottom of the stem. Break away the green outer leaves until you reach the tender yellow leaves. Using a paring knife, trim the heart and stem, cutting downward from the base of the leaves to the end of the stem, creating a smooth line. Cut the artichoke lengthwise in half. Using a sharp spoon, scoop out the fuzzy choke. Place the cleaned artichoke in the lemon water.

FOR THE ZUCCHINI

Cut off the ends of the zucchini and pat dry. Cut each zucchini in half, then use a mandoline or a chef's knife to slice the zucchini lengthwise into ¼-inch-thick slices. Cut the lengths into ¼-inch-thick "french fries."

FOR THE LAMB CHOPS

One at a time, place each lamb chop between two sheets of plastic wrap and pound the meat gently, avoiding the bone, with a meat tenderizer until it is almost double in diameter. Transfer the chops to a tray and season lightly with salt and pepper. Cover and let rest at room temperature for 10 minutes.

Whisk the eggs in a large bowl and season lightly with salt and pepper. Spread the flour and bread crumbs on separate large plates.

Holding a lamb chop by the bone, dust it with flour on both sides, then dip in the egg, hold it over the bowl to drain the excess, and dredge both sides of the chop in the bread crumbs. Press lightly on the breaded chop with the palm of your hand to help ensure that the crust stays intact during cooking, and transfer to a clean tray. Repeat with the remaining chops.

In a deep fryer or a deep heavy pot, heat the oil to 350°F.

Meanwhile, drain the artichokes and pat dry with paper towels. Bread the artichokes as you did the lamb chops. Place on a plate and set aside. Repeat with the zucchini.

Line a baking sheet with paper towels. Fry the ingredients in batches that allow space for movement in the oil; be sure not to overcrowd the fryer.

Gently place the zucchini, in batches, in the hot oil and cook for 3 to 5 minutes, or until golden brown. Using a slotted spoon, transfer to the prepared baking sheet. Set aside in a warm spot. Use a skimmer to remove any breading that falls into the oil as you work.

Continued

Gently place the artichokes in the hot oil, again in batches, and cook for 5 to 6 minutes, or until tender in the middle and golden brown. Transfer to the prepared pan.

Fry the lamb chops, turning once, for about 4 minutes per side, or until the meat is medium-rare and the crust is crisp and brown. Using a spatula, transfer the chops to the pan with the vegetables. Use paper towels to blot any excess oil from the chops and vegetables.

Arrange the fritto misto on a platter and serve with lemon wedges.

EASTER LAMB
Agnello Pasquale

EASTER IS OUR BIGGEST FEAST, comparable to Thanksgiving in America. At my house, we fasted the day before Easter, in keeping with religious tradition. We would cook up plenty of eggs, wrapping them in onion skins and flowers and then boiling them. In this way, they acquired rich color which made for beautiful accents for dinner the next day. The priest came to our house to bless the eggs (and anything else we wanted him to bless!). Alongside the eggs on the Easter table, we put some olive branches, also blessed by the priest. The main course was the Paschal lamb. This recipe, which includes a lamb stew and a separately cooked rack of lamb, all garnished with fried artichokes, has been in my family for generations. The only thing I have omitted is the split and roasted lamb's head. Consuming it was an honor reserved for the men in the family. I am sorry that this custom has not transplanted well across the Atlantic.

2½ pounds boneless lamb shoulder, trimmed of excess fat and cut into ½-inch cubes

Kosher salt and freshly ground black pepper

12 tablespoons (6 ounces) unsalted butter

¼ pound pancetta, cut into ¼-inch dice

1 medium onion, thinly sliced

4 garlic cloves, thinly sliced

1 sprig thyme

1 sprig rosemary

4 cups dry white wine, such as Verdicchio or Pinot Grigio

4 cups Chicken Stock (page 214)

2½ quarts sunflower or peanut oil

1 rack of lamb, 7 or 8 chops

Juice of ½ lemon

12 baby artichokes

4 large eggs

½ cup dry bread crumbs

¾ cup freshly grated Parmigiano-Reggiano

3 tablespoons grated lemon zest

¼ cup finely chopped Italian parsley

Continued

Lightly season the lamb shoulder with salt and pepper. Put on a plate and let stand at room temperature for 20 minutes.

In a Dutch oven or other large heavy pot, melt 6 tablespoons of the butter over medium-high heat. Add the pancetta and sauté for 4 to 5 minutes, or until it begins to crisp. Add the onion, garlic, thyme, and rosemary and cook for about 10 minutes, or until the onion is soft and translucent. Remove from the heat and set aside.

Place a colander over a medium bowl. Melt the remaining 6 tablespoons butter in a large sauté pan over medium-high heat. Working in small batches so as not to overcrowd the pan, add the cubed lamb and sauté for about 3 to 4 minutes, or until the meat has browned. Transfer to the colander to drain. When all the lamb is browned and drained, add to the pot with the onions.

Set the pot over medium-high heat and cook for 5 minutes, stirring occasionally with a wooden spoon. Add the wine and use a wooden spatula or spoon to scrape any caramelized bits from the bottom of the pot. Reduce the heat to a simmer and cook until the wine has reduced by two-thirds.

Meanwhile, heat the chicken stock in a medium saucepan.

Ladle the warm stock into the pot and quickly bring to a simmer. Reduce the heat to low and let the stew cook gently for about 1 hour and 20 minutes, or until the lamb is very tender. (The stew can be made ahead. Remove from the heat and cool to room temperature, then cover and refrigerate for up to 1 day.)

Twenty minutes before cooking, remove the rack of lamb and the stew (if made ahead) from the refrigerator. Season the rack with salt and pepper and set aside.

Preheat the oven to 375°F. In a deep fryer or a deep heavy pot, heat the oil to 350°F.

FOR THE ARTICHOKES

Combine the lemon juice with 4 cups water in a large bowl. Working with 1 artichoke at a time, cut off ¼ inch from the top of the artichoke and discard. Cut off the bottom of the stem. Break away the green outer leaves until you reach the tender yellow leaves. Using a paring knife, trim the heart and stem, cutting downward from the base of the leaves to the end of the stem, creating a smooth line. Cut the artichoke lengthwise in half. Using a spoon, scoop out the fuzzy choke. Place the cleaned heart in the lemon water.

FOR THE RACK OF LAMB

To cook the rack of lamb, heat a large cast-iron skillet or heavy ovenproof sauté pan over medium-high heat. Place the rack fat side down in the pan and brown the meat in its own fat, about 4 minutes on each side.

Turn the rack fat side up, transfer the pan to the oven, and roast for about 8 minutes, or until it reaches an internal temperature of 125°F, for medium-rare. Transfer the lamb to a platter, cover with aluminum foil, and let rest for 10 to 12 minutes.

Meanwhile, gently warm the stew over medium-low heat.

In a bowl, thoroughly mix the eggs, bread crumbs, Parmigiano, and lemon zest. Season lightly with salt and pepper, and set aside.

While the lamb rests, cook the artichokes:

Line a baking sheet with paper towels. Drain the artichokes and pat dry. Using a slotted spoon, place the artichokes, in batches, in the hot oil and cook for about 3 minutes, or until lightly golden. Transfer the artichokes to the prepared baking sheet. Blot with paper towels and season with a little salt.

Just before serving, remove the stew from the heat. Mix in the egg mixture and stir until the sauce thickens. If the sauce doesn't thicken, warm it slightly over very low heat; do not overheat, or the eggs will scramble.

Spoon the stew into a large serving dish. Slice the rack into individual chops and arrange around the stew. Garnish with the artichokes and sprinkle with the parsley. Serve immediately.

Rabbit with Wild Fennel
Coniglio in Porchetta

MOST AMERICANS ASSUME that *porchetta* always means a pork dish. Not true. While a porchetta sandwich of wood-roasted pork seasoned with fennel is the result of the happy combination of a hog with fire, the term *porchetta* actually refers to anything roasted over a wood fire with wild fennel. You can find duck porchetta, sea bass porchetta, and, in this dish, rabbit porchetta. Wild fennel bears the same relationship to farmed fennel that wild strawberries or blueberries do to their cultivated versions. The wild plant is more petite, more intense, more . . . well, "wild." Many regions in Italy claim to be the home of porchetta, but as a Marchigiani chef I cannot let this go unchallenged. A tradition of wood-fired cooking and the presence of wild fennel is Marchigiani to the core.

In this porchetta-style dish of rabbit, the meat is actually braised in a fennel-infused broth flavored with pancetta. (If wild fennel is not available, dill makes a reasonable substitute.)

1 rabbit, about 2½ pounds, cut into 8 pieces: 2 legs, 2 thighs, and 4 breast pieces (you can have the butcher do this)

Kosher salt and freshly ground black pepper

4 cups water

1¼ cups wild fennel sprigs or about 1 bunch dill

½ cup extra virgin olive oil

3 garlic cloves, peeled

½ pound pancetta, cut into ¼-inch dice

2 cups dry white wine, such as Verdicchio or Pinot Grigio

Lightly season the rabbit with salt and pepper. Set aside on a plate.

Bring the water to a boil in a medium saucepan. Pick the fronds from the fennel (or dill) stems and place in a small bowl; set aside. Add the stems to the boiling water. Boil for 3 minutes, then remove from the heat. Cover the pan and let steep for 20 minutes. Strain the liquid and set aside; discard the stems.

Set a large Dutch oven or other pot big enough to hold the rabbit pieces in a single layer over medium heat. Add the oil and garlic. When the garlic cloves are golden brown, remove them and discard. Add the rabbit to the pot and sear for about 3 minutes per side, or until golden.

Add the pancetta and sauté for an additional 3 minutes, or until it begins to crisp. Add the wine and use a wooden spatula or spoon to scrape the bottom of the pan to loosen the browned bits. Let the wine simmer until it has almost completely evaporated.

Add 1½ cups of the reserved fennel liquid, and reduce the heat to medium-low. Cover and simmer for about 1 hour and 20 minutes, or until the rabbit is very tender and the meat pulls away from the bone easily. Check the pot from time to time and add more fennel water as needed to maintain about ½ inch of liquid at all times.

Transfer the rabbit to a serving platter, and spoon the pan juices over and around it. Chop the fennel fronds, sprinkle them over the rabbit, and serve.

Desserts

CRISPY FRIED PASTRY CREAM SQUARES
Crema Fritta

❀ *Makes 48 pieces*

IT IS HARD TO IMAGINE a Marchigiani feast without these crispy creamy, sweet fried nuggets. Crema fritta is served as a dessert or as a sweet snack; it is also part of a traditional Ascoli fritto misto (see page 168), along with olives Ascolana. My Aunt Emilia made irresistible crema fritta. Never in my life was I able to eat just one of hers.

At home, my wife, Maria, and I love to have this as a treat after the kids have gone to sleep. Maria will make the best Spanish omelet in the world, and I'll do the crema fritta. With a cold sweet wine, you have the beginnings of a great romantic evening.

2 cups whole milk	¾ cup Italian 00 flour or all-purpose flour
2 cups heavy cream	
Zest of 1 lemon, removed in long strips with a vegetable peeler (yellow part only)	½ cup cornstarch
	¼ cup Italian anise liqueur, such as Mistra Varnelli, or anisette
Zest of 1 orange, removed in long strips with a vegetable peeler (orange part only)	3 quarts sunflower or peanut oil
1¾ cups granulated sugar	8 large eggs
24 large egg yolks	2¾ cups dried bread crumbs

Combine the milk, cream, and lemon and orange zest in a large saucepan and slowly bring to a simmer over low heat. Add 1 cup of the sugar and stir until the sugar has completely dissolved. Remove the pan from the heat, cover tightly, and let steep for 20 minutes.

Meanwhile, in a standing mixer fitted with a whisk, whisk the yolks and the remaining ¾ cup sugar for about 4 minutes, or until smooth and light. Sift the flour and cornstarch into the egg mixture and whisk until completely incorporated.

Strain the infused milk mixture through a fine-mesh strainer into another large saucepan. Place the pan over medium-high heat and bring to a boil.

Remove from the heat. Temper the egg mixture by slowly adding about ½ cup milk to the eggs, whisking constantly. Return the egg mixture to the saucepan, whisking constantly. Set the pan over low heat and whisk vigorously until the cream thickens and begins to simmer. Switch from the whisk to a wooden spatula or spoon and continue stirring for about 4 minutes, until the mixture becomes a thick custard.

Immediately transfer the cream to a bowl. Add the liqueur and mix well. Pour the cream into a 9-by-13-inch baking dish and spread evenly. Let cool, then cover with plastic wrap and refrigerate overnight.

In a deep fryer or deep heavy pot, heat the oil to 350°F. Whisk the eggs in a large shallow bowl. Spread the bread crumbs on a plate.

Cut the pastry cream into 1½-inch squares, dipping the knife in hot water and wiping it dry between cuts. Dip the squares into the eggs, let the excess drain over the bowl, and then dredge in the bread crumbs to coat on all sides. Place on a plate.

Line a baking sheet with paper towels. Using a slotted spoon, carefully drop the pastry cream squares, in batches, into the hot oil and fry, turning once, for 2 to 3 minutes per side, or until golden and crisp. Place the fried squares on the prepared baking sheet and blot off excess oil with paper towels. Serve warm or at room temperature. These are best served right after frying, but if necessary, the cooled fried cream can be refrigerated in an airtight container for up to 1 day.

Vanilla Honey Custard

Lattarolo

I LEARNED THIS RECIPE from our landlady in Osimo, Ghiga Diotavelli. She and her sister, Jolanda, owned our apartment building. Their home was filled with antique furniture, old paintings, and pretty silver, but when I think of them, it is not as rich ladies, but rather two sweet women who took an interest in helping me learn to cook. (In fact, they were so nice that when I was very young I thought they were my grandmothers.) Every time I taste this custard, I think of Ghiga and me in the kitchen, with Jolanda reciting poetry in the adjoining dining room.

1 quart whole milk	6 large egg yolks
1 tablespoon grated lemon zest	½ cup honey
5 coffee beans	
1 cinnamon stick	**Caramel**
2 vanilla beans	½ cup granulated sugar
2 large eggs	2 tablespoons water

Position a rack in the center of the oven and preheat the oven to 275°F.

Pour the milk into a medium saucepan and set over low heat. Add the zest, coffee beans, and cinnamon stick. Using a paring knife, split the vanilla beans, scrape the seeds into the milk, and drop in the pods. Bring to a simmer and simmer to reduce the milk by half, about 25 minutes.

Strain the milk through a fine-mesh strainer. Remove the pods from the strainer and, with a paring knife, scrape any remaining seeds into the milk.

Mix the eggs, yolks, and honey in a medium bowl. Gradually add the milk, whisking constantly.

For the caramel: Stir the sugar and water together in a small saucepan. Bring to a boil over medium-high heat, stirring to dissolve the sugar. Cook, without stirring, until the caramel is amber in color. Pour into a

9-×-5-inch loaf pan, and tilt the pan to spread the caramel evenly over the bottom. Set aside on a rack at room temperature for 5 to 6 minutes, or until the caramel sets.

Pour the custard into the caramel-lined pan. Place the pan in a large baking dish and add enough room-temperature water to come halfway up the sides of the pan. Cover the baking dish and pan with a large sheet of aluminum foil.

Bake the custard for 1 hour, or until it has set but the center is still a little loose, like jelly. Remove from the oven and let the custard cool completely in the water bath. Remove from the water, cover, and refrigerate overnight.

To serve, dip the pan briefly in hot water to loosen the caramel, then unmold onto a rimmed serving platter. Cut into slices and arrange on individual plates.

APPLE FRITTERS
Fritelle di Mele

MY NONNA PALMINA was known as one of the best cooks in Santo Stefano (maybe that's where my dad and I got our cooking DNA). I remember her as a tiny old lady with small hands and snow-white hair that she tied up in a bun. She could turn out a big family dinner with many courses, yet she never hurried, never rushed. She made it seem effortless and her food had similar grace and ease. Every autumn she would wait until apples were at their peak, and then it was time for these incomparable fritters.

Apples

4 Honey Gold, Golden Delicious, or Liberty apples

½ cinnamon stick

½ cup granulated sugar

2 tablespoons Italian anise liqueur, such as Mistra Varnelli, or anisette

Batter

2 large eggs, separated

2 large egg yolks

¼ cup granulated sugar

¼ cup sparkling water, such as Pellegrino

¾ cup Italian oo flour or all-purpose flour

1½ teaspoons baking powder

3 tablespoons (1½ ounces) unsalted butter, melted

Grated zest of 1 lemon

Grated zest of 1 orange

2 tablespoons Italian anise liqueur, such as Mistra Varnelli, or Anisette

3 quarts sunflower or peanut oil

Confectioners' sugar for dusting

FOR THE APPLES

With an apple corer, core the apples. Slice them into ¼-inch-thick rings.

Grate the cinnamon stick (a Microplane grater works well) into a small bowl. Add the sugar and toss to mix. Place the apples in a shallow baking pan and dust them with the sugar mixture, turning to coat both sides. Sprinkle with the liqueur. Cover and let the apples macerate for 6 hours.

In a large bowl, whisk the yolks with 2 tablespoons of the sugar. Add the water, flour, baking powder, butter, lemon and orange zests, and liqueur and whisk for about 5 minutes, or until the batter is creamy. Cover the bowl and let stand at room temperature for 1 hour.

In a deep fryer or deep heavy pot, heat the oil to 350°F.

In a medium bowl, whip the whites with the remaining 2 tablespoons sugar until soft peaks form. Gently fold the whites into the batter.

Line a plate with paper towels. Dry the apples with paper towels. Using the handle of a wooden spoon, lift one apple ring by the hole and dip in the batter. Shake off any excess and gently slide it in the hot oil. Add only as many more slices as fit comfortably in the fryer. Cook 2 to 3 minutes per side, or until golden brown. Transfer the fritters to the lined plate, blot up any excess oil, and dust with confectioners' sugar. Repeat with the remaining apple slices. Serve immediately.

CARNIVAL FRITTERS
Scroccafusi

❋ *Makes about 150 fritters*

WHEN I WAS FIFTEEN, I worked every weekend in a pastry shop outside Osimo. My father bought me a bike so I could get to work without his having to drive me there. My day would start at two in the morning: I cracked six hundred eggs, rolled out a thousand croissants, made a hundred fruit cakes and then fried up the scroccafusi that would be sold in all the local shops and bars. Yet even with those memories of all that hard work, I still can eat scroccafusi by the handful.

5 large eggs	¼ cup extra virgin olive oil
1 large egg yolk	3¼ cups Italian oo flour or all-purpose
2 cups granulated sugar	flour
1½ teaspoons grated lemon zest	1 tablespoon ground cinnamon
1½ teaspoons grated orange zest	3 quarts sunflower or peanut oil
3 tablespoons light rum	

Combine the eggs, yolk, and 1 cup of the sugar in the bowl of a standing mixer fitted with the whisk attachment. Beat at low speed until fully blended. Increase the speed to medium and whisk for about 8 minutes, or until the batter is light, airy, and pale. Add the lemon and orange zests, rum, and olive oil and whisk for 1 minute.

Switch to the paddle attachment. Mixing on low speed, slowly add the flour. Once all the flour is incorporated, mix the dough at low speed for 10 minutes longer.

Transfer the dough to a pastry bag fitted with a 1-inch plain tip. Place on a plate and refrigerate for 6 hours.

Bring a large pot of water to a rolling boil. In a deep fryer or deep heavy pot, heat the sunflower oil to 350°F. Lightly oil a baking sheet. Line a second sheet with paper towels.

Combine the remaining 1 cup sugar and the cinnamon in a shallow bowl. Set aside.

When the water is boiling, carefully hold the pastry bag horizontally above the water and squeeze the bag until a 1-inch length of dough is visible. Cut it off with a dinner knife and let it fall into the water. Repeat to make 5 to 7 more fritters. Once they rise to the surface, use a slotted spoon to transfer them to the oiled baking sheet. Form and blanch the remaining fritters, in batches.

Again working in batches, fry the fritters a second time in the hot oil for about 3 to 4 minutes, or until golden brown. Remove to the pan lined with paper towels and blot off any excess oil.

Roll the scroccafusi in the cinnamon sugar, transfer them to a platter, and serve warm.

CHILDREN'S CRESCIA
Crescia dei Bambini

CRESCIA ARE FRIED rounds of dough flavored with orange and lemon zest and dredged—or, actually, buried—in clouds of confectioners' sugar. When we were growing up, my sister and I loved them—but they presented a problem, because if you weren't careful, the sugar and oil would get on your schoolbooks or your clothes. My father always gave me strict orders not to let go of Claudia's hand when she went with me to Mr. Sopranzetti's bakery. So every day on the way to school, I would go into the bakery, and I would hold up a few fingers on my free hand to show how many crescia I wanted. Mr. Sopranzetti's wife, Mariella, would put them in my backpack (again, so I didn't have to let go of Claudia's hand), and then I would reach into my pocket and pay, still holding onto Claudia.

My young son, Luca, has followed in his father's footsteps and eats these as fast as I can make them. You can halve the recipe to make 16 crescia, if you prefer—but I don't think you will have any leftovers!

4 cups Italian oo flour or all-purpose flour	½ cup Italian anise liqueur, such as Mistra Varnelli, or anisette
1 teaspoon baking powder	1 tablespoon grated orange zest
½ teaspoon kosher salt	1 tablespoon grated lemon zest
1½ cups granulated sugar	4 tablespoons (2 ounces) unsalted butter, at room temperature
¼ cup whole milk, at room temperature	3 quarts sunflower or peanut oil
¾ cup room-temperature water	

Sift the flour and baking powder into the bowl of a standing mixer fitted with the dough hook. Add the salt and ½ cup of the sugar.

Combine the milk, water, anise liqueur, and orange and lemon zests in a small pitcher or liquid measuring cup. With the mixer on medium speed, slowly add the liquid ingredients to the flour mixture. Add the butter and mix until it is fully absorbed. Knead the dough for about 8 minutes, or until it pulls away from the sides of the bowl and is smooth and elastic.

Transfer the dough to a bowl and cover with a kitchen towel. Let rest in the refrigerator for at least 6 hours, or overnight.

Turn the dough out onto a countertop or pastry board dusted with flour. Divide the dough into 32 small balls, about 2 inches in diameter. Place on a plate, cover with a kitchen towel, and let rest for 30 minutes.

In a deep fryer or a wide heavy pot, heat the oil to 350°F. Spread the remaining 1 cup sugar in a shallow bowl that is at least 7 inches in diameter, or spread it on a plate.

Line a baking sheet with paper towels.

Dust a little more flour onto your work surface. Using a rolling pin, roll each ball into a disk about 6 inches in diameter and ⅛ inch thick (be sure the size you roll will fit into your fryer), then prick the surface of each disk all over with a fork. Shape a few disks to start, then, once you start frying the crescia, roll out the remaining disks as the first batches cook.

Very carefully place a crescia in the hot oil. As it hits the oil, the baking powder in the dough will cause it to bubble up, and the oil may spurt, so be especially careful. Use the back of a wooden spoon with a long handle to keep the dough submerged in the oil and fry, turning once, for about 2 to 3 minutes per side, or until golden. Using tongs, transfer the crescia to the prepared baking sheet. Blot off excess oil, and dip both sides of the crescia into the sugar. Repeat with the remaining crescia, and serve warm.

PASTRY CREAM TART
Crostata di Crema

❋ Serves 6

ONE OF THE FIRST RECIPES I ever attempted was from the *Italian Talisman Cookbook*, by Ada Boni. It was kind of an Italian *Joy of Cooking*. I decided to start with the recipe for *pasta frolla*, a rich pastry dough, to make a pie. The first results were a disaster, as was my pastry cream. But I stayed with it, trying to improve it: I increased the amount of vanilla and sugar in the pastry cream and used egg yolks instead of whole eggs. It was probably my first attempt at thinking things through like a chef. I worked on the recipe until I had used up all the flour, eggs, butter, and sugar in the house. Here is the version I make today.

Dough

4 cups Italian oo flour or all-purpose flour

1 cup granulated sugar

¾ pound (3 sticks) cold unsalted butter, cubed

1½ teaspoons grated orange zest

1½ teaspoons grated lemon zest

4 large egg yolks

2½ tablespoons plus 1½ teaspoons honey

Pastry Cream

2 cups whole milk

Zest of ½ orange, removed in long strips with a vegetable peeler (orange part only)

Zest of ½ lemon, removed in long strips with a vegetable peeler (yellow part only)

2 vanilla beans

¾ cup granulated sugar, plus more for sprinkling

7 large egg yolks

2 tablespoons cornstarch

FOR THE DOUGH

Sift the flour into the bowl of a standing mixer fitted with the paddle attachment. Add the sugar, butter, and orange and lemon zests. Mix on low speed for about 5 minutes, or until the dough has the consistency of wet sand. Add the egg yolks one at a time, then add the honey and mix until the dough just holds together.

Sprinkle a work surface with flour. Turn the dough out onto the work surface. Dust your hands with flour and knead the dough for 1 minute. Divide the dough in half and shape each half into a disk. Wrap each piece in plastic wrap and refrigerate overnight to allow the dough to relax.

FOR THE PASTRY CREAM

Combine the milk and zest strips in a medium saucepan and set over medium-low heat. Using a paring knife, split the vanilla beans and scrape the seeds into the milk, then drop in the pods. Bring the milk to a boil, and remove from the heat. Cover tightly and let steep for 1 hour.

Strain the milk through a fine-mesh strainer; discard the zest and vanilla beans. Return the milk to the clean saucepan, add half the sugar, and bring to a simmer over medium-high heat.

Meanwhile, in a large bowl, whisk the yolks and the remaining sugar together. Add the cornstarch and whisk until well blended.

To temper the eggs, gradually add about ½ cup of the simmering milk to the egg mixture, whisking constantly. Whisking constantly, slowly add the egg mixture to the simmering milk. Cook, whisking, until the mixture begins to simmer. Exchange the whisk for a wooden spatula or spoon and stir the pastry cream constantly until it boils and begins to thicken. Continue to whisk vigorously for 4 to 5 minutes, or until it has become a thick custard; be sure to scrape the bottom and edges of the pan to prevent scorching.

Immediately transfer the pastry cream to a bowl or other container. Sprinkle the top with about 2 tablespoons of sugar, to prevent a skin from forming. Let cool to room temperature, then cover and refrigerate.

Butter and flour a fluted 12-inch tart pan with a removable bottom.

Continued

Dust a work surface (marble is best) with flour. Remove one piece of the dough from the refrigerator and quickly flatten it with the palm of your hand (this will warm up the dough, making it more malleable). Using a rolling pin, roll the dough into a 14-inch round about ¼ inch thick. To keep it from sticking to the work surface, run a palette knife or long metal spatula under the dough as necessary.

Transfer the dough to the tart pan: Gently ease it down into the pan's corners, without stretching it, and use your fingertips to mold the dough to the fluted sides of the pan. Roll the rolling pin over the top of the pan to remove excess dough. Place in the freezer for 30 minutes.

Position a rack in the middle of the oven and preheat the oven to 375°F.

Prick the bottom of the crust all over with a fork. Bake for 10 to 12 minutes, or until golden and firm. Place on a cooling rack to cool to room temperature. (Leave the oven on.)

Roll out the remaining dough to a 13- to 14-inch round. Using a fluted pastry cutter or a sharp knife, cut into ½-inch-wide ribbons.

Spoon the pastry cream into the cooled crust. Smooth the surface with an offset or rubber spatula. To make an easy lattice crust, arrange half the dough ribbons about 1 inch apart on top of the pastry cream. Lay the remaining strips diagonally across the first ones, placing them 1 inch apart.

Bake for 20 minutes, or until the crust is golden brown. Transfer to the cooling rack and cool to room temperature before unmolding. Serve at room temperature.

ZUPPA INGLESE

ZUPPA INGLESE literally means "English Soup," although it's not soup and it's not really English. Supposedly a chef in Naples created this recipe for Lady Emma Hamilton, known to history as Lord Nelson's mistress. The original recipe calls for a syrup based on a liquor known as Alchermes, which is made from rose petals, sugar, orange, vanilla, aromatic spices, and cochineal (a red dye made from dried insects). Although Marsala, which is easier to find, makes a perfectly acceptable substitute, the color will not be as striking as the original dessert, which had the same captivating blush that the hero of Trafalgar admired in his paramour.

Sponge Cake
½ cup cake flour

½ cup cornstarch

¼ teaspoon kosher salt

6 large eggs

¾ cup granulated sugar

1 tablespoon grated orange zest

Pastry Cream
1 quart whole milk

2 vanilla beans

1½ cups granulated sugar

13 large egg yolks

½ cup cornstarch

1½ cups finely chopped semisweet
   chocolate (about 8 ounces)

Syrup
¾ cup water

½ cup granulated sugar

1½ cups Alchermes or Marsala

Whipped cream for serving

Fresh berries for serving

FOR THE SPONGE CAKE

Position a rack in the middle of the oven and preheat the oven to 375°F. Butter and flour a 12-inch round cake pan or springform pan.

Sift the flour, cornstarch, and salt onto a sheet of parchment paper. Set aside.

Continued

Place the eggs in the bowl of a standing mixer fitted with the whisk attachment. Whip at medium speed until blended. Still whipping on medium speed, add the sugar in a slow, steady stream. Add the zest. Increase to high speed and whip for about 10 minutes, or until the mixture is light, airy, and pale.

Remove the bowl from the mixer and fold in the flour mixture. Pour the batter into the prepared pan and level smooth the top with an offset or rubber spatula.

Bake for 10 minutes, or until golden. Transfer the cake to a rack and cool for 5 minutes, then unmold onto the rack and cool to room temperature.

MEANWHILE, FOR THE PASTRY CREAM

Warm the milk in a large saucepan over medium-low heat. Using a paring knife, split the vanilla beans and scrape the seeds into the warm milk, then add the split pods. Add ¾ cup of the sugar to the saucepan. Bring to a boil, stirring to dissolve the sugar, and remove from the heat. Cover tightly and let steep for 1 hour.

When the cake is completely cool, wrap it in plastic wrap and freeze for 1 hour, to make it easier to slice into layers.

Strain the infused milk through a fine-mesh strainer into the cleaned saucepan; discard the vanilla pods. Bring the milk to a simmer over medium-low heat.

Meanwhile, in a bowl, whisk together the yolks and the remaining ¾ cup sugar. Sift in the cornstarch and whisk until smooth. Ladle about ½ cup of the simmering milk into the egg mixture, whisking vigorously. Whisking constantly, add the eggs in a slow, steady stream to the hot milk.

Return the pan to medium-low heat and whisk until the mixture is creamy and begins to simmer. Exchange the whisk for a wooden spatula or spoon, increase the heat to medium-high heat, and stir the pastry cream gently but constantly until it boils and begins to thicken. Continue to mix vigorously for 4 to 5 minutes, or until it has become a thick custard; be sure to scrape the bottom and edges of the pan to prevent scorching. Remove the pan from the heat and divide the pastry cream between two bowls. Immediately add the chocolate to one of the bowls and stir gently until the chocolate has melted and is fully incorporated. Cover both bowls and set aside to cool.

FOR THE SYRUP

Bring the water to a boil in a small saucepan. Remove from the heat, add the sugar and Marsala, and stir until the sugar has dissolved. Let cool until warm.

If you don't have a trifle bowl, choose a round serving dish 10 to 12 inches in diameter and 2 inches deep. Using a long serrated knife, slice the cake into 3 layers. Place the first layer in the bottom of the bowl. Using a pastry brush, soak the cake with one-third of the syrup. Spread half of the vanilla pastry cream on top of the cake. Lay a second layer of cake on the pastry cream and brush with half the remaining syrup. Spread all of the chocolate pastry cream on top of the cake. Place the final layer of cake on top and brush with the remaining syrup. Spread the remaining vanilla pastry cream over the top. Refrigerate for at least 6 hours, or overnight.

Serve the cake cold, with whipped cream and berries.

BOSTRENGO RICE CAKE

Bostrengo

THE BAKERS OF SANT 'ANGELO IN VADO turn out thousands of these rice cakes for the annual Festival of Bostrengo on August 16, when people come from all over Italy. We usually had our cakes a little later in the year, when my family would take a Sunday drive north to Vado to get a few truffles. For Claudia and me, the rice cakes, not the truffles, were the highlight of the journey. Made with milk, honey, rice, eggs, lemon, chocolate, and a cornucopia of fruits, they had a heavenly texture and taste. Although the rule was no eating in the car, Claudia and I couldn't resist, and my father would pretend he didn't see us as we indulged ourselves.

1 cup Carnaroli or Arborio rice

6 thin slices dense white bread, crusts removed and cut into ¼-inch cubes

½ cup whole milk

2 cups granulated sugar

¼ cup water

2 vanilla beans

4½ cups diced (¼-inch) peeled Golden Delicious apples (about 2 pounds apples)

4 cups diced (¼-inch) peeled Bosc pears (about 2 pounds pears)

1¼ cups Italian oo flour or all-purpose flour

1¾ cups unsweetened cocoa powder

1 tablespoon baking powder

½ pound (2 sticks) unsalted butter, cubed

4 large eggs

½ cup honey

1 tablespoon grated orange zest

1 tablespoon grated lemon zest

⅔ cup light rum

¾ cup espresso or strong coffee

1 cup dark raisins

1 cup coarsely chopped dried figs

Vanilla ice cream or whipped cream (optional)

Bring 4 cups water to a rolling boil in a large saucepan. Add the rice and cook for 15 minutes, or until tender. Drain in a colander and rinse well with cold water to remove some of the starch. Transfer to a small bowl and set aside.

Meanwhile, in a small bowl, combine the bread and milk. Set aside to soak.

Combine 1 cup of the sugar and the ¼ cup water in a large sauté pan. Using a paring knife, split the vanilla beans, scrape the seeds into the sugar, and then drop in the pods. Place the pan over medium-high heat and bring to a boil, stirring to dissolve the sugar. Continue to cook, without stirring, until the caramel is a rich golden amber. Immediately, add the apples and pears and cook for about 5 minutes, or until the fruit softens, stirring occasionally with a wooden spatula or spoon to dissolve any lumps of caramel. Transfer to a baking sheet, spreading out the fruit, and set on a wire cooling rack. Remove the vanilla pods from the pan, and let the caramelized fruit cool to room temperature.

Position the racks in the bottom and middle of the oven and preheat the oven to 350°F.

Sift the flour, cocoa, and baking powder into a bowl. Set aside.

Melt the butter in a saucepan over medium-low heat. Using a pastry brush, butter a 12-inch springform pan. Reserve the remaining butter.

Bring a small ovenproof pot of water to a boil.

Meanwhile, place the eggs in the bowl of a standing mixer fitted with the paddle attachment. Add the remaining 1 cup sugar and mix at medium speed for 5 minutes, or until pale and thick. Add the honey, soaked bread, with any liquid, the orange and lemon zests, rum, and espresso. Mix at medium speed for 2 minutes. Reduce the speed to low, add the flour mixture, and mix just until incorporated. Remove the bowl from the mixer and fold in the remaining melted butter, the raisins, figs, apples, and pears. Fold in the rice.

Pour the batter into the prepared pan. Place the pot of boiling water in one corner of the bottom oven rack, not directly under the springform pan. (The steam will help give the cake a moist texture.) Place the cake on the center rack and bake for 1 hour and 15 minutes, or until a skewer inserted in the center comes out clean.

Transfer the cake to a cooling rack and cool for 20 minutes. Remove the sides of the pan, and let cool to room temperature.

Serve with vanilla ice cream or whipped cream, if desired. Store any leftover cake in the refrigerator; bring to room temperature before serving.

ANISE COOKIES

Ciambelline all'Anice

❁ Makes 100 cookies

ON A SCOUTING TRIP to Le Marche for this book, we were entertained by the charming and amusing mayor of the hill town of Matelica. On a day when spring was in glorious full bloom, he took us for a ride up in the mountains. Mulberry bushes sprouted with new green and the tree we call a Judas plum was a day-glo purple. We zigzagged along endless switchbacks until we came to an isolated green valley crowned by a tiny ancient village.

As we made our way up and down the steps and along the sidewalks of the village, I breathed in deeply and was hit with waves of sweetness, the smell of wild anise and mint. The perfume reminded me so much of the warm sweetness that emanates from bakeries when they make ciambelline, ring-shaped anise cookies.

8 cups Italian 00 flour or all-purpose flour	½ cup Italian anise liqueur, such as Mistra Varnelli, or anisette
2½ cups granulated sugar, plus extra for sprinkling	½ cup anise seeds
1½ cups extra virgin olive oil	1 teaspoon kosher salt
1¼ cups dry white wine, such as Verdicchio or Pinot Grigio	1 teaspoon baking soda
	1 large egg
	3 tablespoons whole milk

Sift the flour into the bowl of a standing mixer fitted with the dough hook. Add the sugar and mix at low speed to combine.

Combine the olive oil, wine, and liqueur in a large measuring cup or a bowl and add to the flour in a slow, steady stream, mixing until fully incorporated. Add the anise seeds, salt, and baking soda and knead the dough for about 20 minutes, or until it pulls away from the sides of the bowl and is smooth and elastic. Turn the dough out onto a plate, cover with a kitchen towel, and let rest for 30 minutes at room temperature.

Position the racks in the upper and lower thirds of the oven and preheat the oven to 375°F. Line two baking sheets with parchment paper.

Lightly dust a counter or pastry board with flour. Be careful not to use too much flour as you are rolling the dough, or the ends will not stick together when you form the rings. Pull off a piece of dough and roll it under the palms of your hands into a rope that is ¾ inch in diameter. Cut the dough into 3-inch lengths. Join the ends of one piece to form a ring shape, transfer to one of the baking sheets, and pinch the seam to seal. Continue forming rings, leaving about ½ inch of space between the cookies, until you have filled the baking sheets.

Mix the egg and milk in a small bowl. Using a pastry brush, lightly brush the cookies with the egg wash, then sprinkle them with sugar. Bake for 10 minutes, rotating the pans once halfway through baking, or until lightly golden. Let cool on the baking sheets for about 2 minutes, then transfer to racks to cool completely. Repeat with the remaining dough. Store the cookies in a sealed container for up to 2 weeks.

Cookies for the Day of the Dead
Fave dei Morti

❊ *Makes 200 cookies*

Most Americans associate the Day of the Dead with Mexico, and pictures of skeletons playing guitars. But the Day of the Dead is also celebrated in Italy, and these cookies, which may be shaped like fava beans (*fave*) or imprinted with their shape, have always been made for that special day. When we were growing up, my sister and I would eat a few of these cookies, and leave a few out overnight to please the souls of the dead. When we awoke in the morning, sure enough, the cookies were gone, which we took as proof of a visitation from beyond the grave.

The cookies can be eaten plain or sandwiched together with a bit of jam or melted chocolate. The filling will soften the cookies, so fill shortly before serving. The recipe makes a lot, but the (unfilled) cookies keep very well.

NOTE When I worked in a pastry shop, I learned a neat shortcut: Instead of waiting for cold egg whites to come to room temperature, simply whisk the whites in a metal bowl set over a pot of simmering water—they will come up to room temperature rapidly. As soon as the egg whites are at room temperature, remove the bowl and proceed with your recipe.

5 large egg whites	¼ cup light rum
2½ cups granulated sugar	2 tablespoons manteca (soft lard; see
4 cups almond flour (see Sources, page	Sources, page 223), at room
223)	temperature
2 teaspoons ground cinnamon	¼ cup confectioners' sugar for dusting

Put the egg whites in the bowl of a standing mixer, set the bowl over a pot of hot water, and whisk until they are at room temperature. Add about one-third of the sugar to the bowl and attach the bowl to the mixer stand. Using the whisk attachment, beat at medium speed for 4 minutes. Add another one-third of the sugar and whisk for 4 minutes. Add the remaining sugar and whisk for an additional 2 minutes, or until the whites form stiff peaks.

Remove the bowl from the mixer and, using a large rubber spatula, fold in the almond flour, the cinnamon, and the rum, working gently from the bottom of the bowl to the top. When the flour is fully incorporated, add the lard and continue to fold just until it is incorporated.

Line two or more baking sheets with parchment paper.

Transfer the dough to a pastry bag fitted with a ¼-inch plain tip. Pipe 1-inch round cookies that are about ¼ inch high onto the lined baking sheets, leaving 2 inches of space between them.

Moisten your finger and make an indentation that looks like a fava bean in the center of each cookie. Dust the cookies with confectioners' sugar and let stand, uncovered, in a well-ventilated area for 45 minutes. The tops will form a slight crust.

Position the racks in the center and lower third of the oven and preheat the oven to 350°F.

Bake the cookies for about 10 minutes, rotating the pans once halfway through baking, or until they form a crisp crust. Let the cookies cool to room temperature on the pans on wire racks. Store in airtight containers for up to 2 days.

WINE MUST POLENTA
Polenta di Mosto

❈ *Serves 6*

ONCE THE GRAPES have been pressed for wine in the fall, what's left in the wine press is known as must. After the harvest, it was used in this dessert found all over Le Marche. It was often prepared as a thank-you for the workers in the vineyards. The sweetened polenta was mounded on large platters, sprinkled generously with walnuts, and served at the end of the harvest feast.

You would be hard pressed to come up with a more powerfully flavored dessert than this.

NOTE Wine must is only available during harvesttime. Ask your favorite winemaker or local vineyard if it is possible to purchase some.

1¼ cups granulated sugar, plus extra for sprinkling

1¾ cups white polenta flour (such as Moretti bramata bianca; see Sources, page 223) or finely ground yellow polenta

5 cups wine must

2 cups walnut halves

Combine the sugar and polenta in a medium bowl.

Pour the must into a large saucepan. Bring to a simmer over medium-low heat and simmer until reduced by one-third, to about 3½ cups. Strain the must through a fine-mesh strainer into another large saucepan. Bring back to a simmer over medium-low heat. Whisking constantly, add the sugar and polenta in a slow, thin stream, then continue whisking for 1 minute. Simmer for 1 hour, stirring vigorously with a wooden spatula or spoon every 5 to 10 minutes to prevent lumps.

Pour the warm polenta into a large serving dish. Sprinkle with sugar and the walnuts. The polenta can be served warm, at room temperature, or cold. (Cool to room temperature before refrigerating to serve cold.) Spoon out the warm polenta, or cut the cooled or chilled polenta into wedges or slices.

WALNUT HONEY BREAD

Pane Nociato

❁ *Makes 4 Loaves*

I CANNOT THINK of this rich, sweet bread without summoning up the picture of my Aunt Amelia. It was a tradition to have pane nociato on November 1, the Day of the Dead. Every year, Amelia (she wasn't really my aunt, but such a close friend that we thought of her as family) sat by the window and worked the dough by hand on her wooden table, adding the walnuts, raisins, and mistra, the intense sweet anise liqueur of Le Marche. My sister, Claudia, and I would eat our fill, washed down with cups of milk. The grown-ups would each have a slice along with a glass of vini di viscioli, another Marchigiani liqueur that is a specialty of Pergola. It is made from red wine and a variety of wild cherries known as *Prunus cerasus*.

1¼ cups water	2¾ cups coarsely chopped walnuts
¾ cup whole milk	½ cup Italian anise liqueur, such
12 tablespoons (6 ounces) unsalted butter, cut into 1-inch cubes	as Mistra Varnelli, or anisette
¼ cup active dry yeast	Grated zest of 3 lemons
8½ cups Italian 00 flour or all-purpose flour	1 tablespoon ground cinnamon
	3 tablespoons anise seeds, finely ground in a spice grinder
1¾ cups honey	¼ teaspoon kosher salt

Combine the water, milk, and butter in a medium saucepan and warm over low heat until the mixture reaches 105° to 115°F. Remove from the heat, add the yeast, and stir until the yeast has dissolved.

Sift the flour into the bowl of a standing mixer fitted with the dough hook. Mixing at low speed, slowly add the milk mixture, mixing until the liquid has been completely absorbed. Increase the speed to medium and knead the dough for about 15 minutes, or until it is smooth, elastic, and no longer sticky.

Continued

Dust a large bowl with flour. Place the dough in the bowl and cover the bowl with a damp towel. Let the dough rise in a warm place for about 4 hours, or until doubled in size.

Return the dough to the mixer, again fitted with the dough hook. Add the honey, walnuts, liqueur, lemon zest, cinnamon, anise, and salt and mix on low speed until fully incorporated.

Butter two baking sheets and dust with flour. Dust a work surface with flour. Place the dough on the work surface, and divide it into 4 pieces. Shape each piece into a loaf about 12 to 14 inches long, and place 2 loaves on each baking sheet. Let rise, uncovered, in a warm spot for 3 hours, or until doubled in size.

Position the racks in the upper and lower thirds of the oven and preheat the oven to 350°F.

Bake the bread for about 45 minutes, switching the position of the baking sheets halfway through, until the crust is golden brown and a metal skewer or toothpick inserted into the center of a loaf comes out dry and slightly warm. Transfer to a rack and let cool before slicing.

Sweet Orange and Raisin Bread
Ciambella

❉ *Serves 8 to 12*

CIAMBELLA IS UNQUESTIONABLY the most popular dessert in all of Le Marche. Farm women would bring slices of ciambella to the men working in the field as a *merenda* (midafternoon snack). Every housewife had her own secret recipe that she believed to be the best. You could probably fill a book with the different ways to make Marchigiani ciambella: how much anise, which dried fruit, how much it was kneaded, what shape it was (sometimes it is baked as a ring), etc. I loved the way our local baker, Mr. Sopranzetti, stuffed his with chocolate.

1 ½ cups dark raisins

1 ½ cups finely diced candied orange peel

½ cup Italian anise liqueur, such as Mistra Varnelli, or anisette

7 cups Italian 00 flour or bread flour

2 tablespoons baking powder

¾ pound (3 sticks) unsalted butter, softened

1¾ cups granulated sugar, plus extra for sprinkling

15 large egg yolks

Grated zest of 3 lemons

Grated zest of 4 oranges

1½ cups whole milk

Combine the raisins and candied orange in a small bowl, pour in the liqueur, and let soak for 30 minutes.

Position a rack in the center of the oven and preheat the oven to 350°F.

Line a baking sheet with parchment paper.

Sift the flour and baking powder into a bowl, and set aside.

Combine the butter and sugar in the bowl of a standing mixer fitted with the paddle attachment and beat on medium speed for 3 to 5 minutes, until smooth and pale. Reduce the speed to low and add the yolks, a few at a time, and then the zests, mixing until incorporated.

Continued

Alternately add the milk and the flour mixture, beginning and ending with the flour. Switch to the dough hook and, with the mixer on low speed, add the raisins and candied orange, with the soaking liquid. Mix until fully incorporated.

Generously flour a work surface. Place the dough on the work surface and shape it into a loaf about 14 inches long. Place it on the prepared pan and sprinkle the top with sugar.

Bake the bread for 40 minutes, or until golden brown. Transfer to a cooling rack, and serve warm or at room temperature.

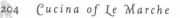

Sweet Rolls with Raisins
Maritozzi

❉ *Makes 24 Rolls*

EVERY BOY CARRIES THE memory of the first woman he thought of as beautiful: Not a mother, not a grandmother, and not a love interest, because this occurs to you at age seven or eight when you don't have an idea in your head why you should be thinking such things. In my life, that first beauty was Fiorella, the owner of a grocery near our house. When I knew she was making these sweet breads on Wednesday afternoons, I always found a way to show up and kick my soccer ball around in the backyard with her kids. The next morning, on my way to school, I would stop in at her store at 7 o'clock and my maritozzo would be there in a bag on the counter waiting for me. By eight o'clock, she was always sold out, which tells you how good those maritozzi were—or, perhaps, how many people shared my opinion about her beauty, or perhaps both.

½ cup Italian anise liqueur, such as Mistra Varnelli, or anisette

1 cup dark raisins

1¼ cups plus 3 tablespoons whole milk

¼ cup active dry yeast

½ cup water

¼ cup honey

7¼ cups Italian 00 flour or bread flour

1½ cups granulated sugar, plus more for sprinkling

14 ounces (3½ sticks) unsalted butter, cut into cubes and softened

1 tablespoon grated orange zest

1 tablespoon grated lemon zest

10 large eggs

2 tablespoons (1 ounce) unsalted butter, melted

Jam or sweetened whipped cream (optional)

Warm the anise liqueur in a small saucepan. Remove from the heat and add the raisins. Set aside to soak.

Warm 1¼ cups of the milk in a small saucepan until it reaches 105° to 115°F. Remove from the heat and add the yeast. Stir until the yeast has fully dissolved. Add the water and honey and mix gently.

Continued

Sift the flour into the bowl of a standing mixer fitted with the dough hook. Add 1 cup of the sugar, the softened butter, and orange and lemon zests. Mix at low speed for 3 to 4 minutes, or until the mixture is like wet sand.

With the mixer on low speed, add 1 egg and mix well, then add more eggs, 2 at a time, mixing after each addition until fully incorporated. Slowly add the milk mixture and continue kneading for about 20 minutes, or until the dough pulls away from the sides of the bowl and is smooth and elastic.

Add the raisins, with their soaking liquid, and mix on low speed for 5 more minutes.

Transfer the dough to a large bowl and cover with a dampened cloth. Let rise in a warm corner of the kitchen for about 3 hours, or until it has doubled in size.

Line four baking sheets with parchment paper. (If you have only two baking sheets, line them, then cut 2 more pieces of parchment the same size and lay them on the counter.) Using a pastry brush, butter the paper with the melted butter. Sprinkle the remaining ½ cup of sugar evenly over the paper.

Dust a counter or pastry board with flour and turn the dough out onto it. Divide the dough into 24 equal pieces. Roll each piece under your palm into a small round roll.

Arrange the rolls on the prepared pans and let them rest in a warm corner of the kitchen for 3 hours, or until doubled in size.

Position the oven racks in the upper and lower thirds of the oven and preheat the oven to 400°F. If you have two ovens (and four baking sheets), you can bake all the rolls at once. Otherwise, bake in batches.

Combine the remaining 1 egg and the 3 tablespoons milk in a small bowl and blend well with a fork. Using a pastry brush, brush the top of each maritozzo with the egg wash. Sprinkle the rolls with sugar.

Bake for about 10 minutes, rotating the pans halfway through baking, or until golden brown. Serve warm, with jam or sweetened whipped cream, if desired.

Basics

Basic Tomato Sauce
Sugo Finto

❀ *Makes about 3 cups*

I INCLUDE THIS RECIPE not because the world needs another tomato sauce recipe, but because the world needs to use more lard! You can use olive oil in place of lard but the taste will not be the same. Our *battuto*—the Italian version of French cooking's "holy trinity" of celery, onion, and carrots—is made with salt pork and rendered lard, rather than the more typical oil.

½ pound salt pork, cut into small pieces	1 celery stalk, finely diced
Two 3-inch sprigs marjoram	¼ cup plus 2 tablespoons tomato paste
Two 3-inch sprigs thyme	1¾ cups water
2 garlic cloves, peeled	Kosher salt and freshly ground
1 onion, finely diced	black pepper
1 carrot, finely diced	

Place the salt pork, leaves from 1 marjoram sprig, leaves from 1 thyme sprig, and garlic on a cutting board and, using a chef's knife, mince the ingredients until they form a uniform paste. (Alternatively, combine the salt pork, marjoram, thyme, and garlic in a food processor and process for 2 minutes.)

Heat a medium or heavy saucepan over medium-high heat. Add the salt pork mixture to the pan. Once it is melted, add the onion, carrot, and celery and cook for about 10 minutes, or until the onion is soft, translucent, and beginning to color. Add the tomato paste and cook, stirring, for 4 minutes to caramelize it.

Gradually stir in the water. Bring to a simmer, reduce the heat, and simmer gently for 30 minutes.

Season the sauce to taste with salt and pepper, remove from the heat, and let stand for 10 minutes.

Chop the leaves from the remaining sprigs of marjoram and thyme, and add to the sauce. Use immediately, or cool, transfer to an airtight container, and refrigerate for up to 2 days.

PASTA DOUGH 1

❋ *Makes about 2 pounds*

PASTA THAT will be stuffed requires a dough that is soft and malleable. I usually make this pasta with sixteen yolks, but for the beginning pasta maker, I find that eighteen yolks result in a more reliably smooth dough. With either number, this is, obviously, a rich dough; the yolks also give it a golden yellow color.

2 cups Italian 00 flour or all-purpose flour	1 teaspoon kosher salt
16 to 18 large egg yolks	2 tablespoons extra virgin olive oil
2 tablespoons whole milk	

Sift the flour into the bowl of a standing mixer fitted with the dough hook. In a large liquid measuring cup, or a bowl with a spout, mix the yolks, milk, salt, and 1 tablespoon of the olive oil. With the mixer running on low speed, slowly pour in the egg mixture and mix until the mixture is completely absorbed. Increase the speed to medium and knead for about 15 minutes, or until the dough pulls away from the sides of the bowl and is smooth and elastic.

Transfer the dough to a plate and massage with the remaining 1 tablespoon olive oil. Cover the dough with a dampened kitchen towel and let rest at room temperature for 2 hours before rolling.

The dough can be refrigerated in a resealable plastic bag for up to 1 day.

Pasta Dough 2

❀ *Makes 1 pound 6 ounces*

Noodles, as opposed to stuffed pastas, require a dough made with some semolina flour. The semolina provides the structure the pasta noodles need to maintain their shape during cooking and the texture that results in the "al dente" bite.

1½ cups Italian 00 flour or all-purpose flour	16 to 18 large egg yolks (see the headnote on page 212)
¼ cup semolina flour	3 tablespoons extra virgin olive oil
1 teaspoon kosher salt	

Sift the two flours into the bowl of a standing mixer fitted with the dough hook. Add the salt. In a large liquid measuring cup or a bowl with a spout, mix the yolks and 2 tablespoons of the olive oil. With the mixer running, slowly pour in the egg mixture and mix until the eggs and oil have been completely absorbed. Increase the speed to medium and knead for about 10 minutes, or until the dough pulls away from the sides of the bowl and is smooth and elastic.

Transfer the dough to a plate and massage with the remaining 1 tablespoon olive oil. Cover the dough with a dampened kitchen towel and let rest at room temperature for 2 hours before rolling.

The dough can be refrigerated in a resealable plastic bag for up to 1 day.

CHICKEN STOCK

❁ *Makes 7 quarts*

2 chickens	3 stalks celery
1 pound chicken necks (optional)	2 medium carrots
½ pound cleaned chicken feet (optional)	2 medium onions, skin left on, cut in half
Pinch of kosher salt	1 small bouquet garni—thyme sprigs,
3½ quarts cold water	Italian parsley stems, and bay leaves
3½ quarts ice cubes	1 tablespoon crushed white peppercorns

Rinse the chickens well, making sure to remove any visible blood. If using, rinse the necks and/or feet well.

Place the chickens, and necks and/or feet, in a large stockpot. Add the salt and water and slowly bring to a simmer over medium heat, skimming well to remove all the impurities that rise to the top.

Add the ice cubes, then skim the fat and any additional impurities that form on the surface. When the liquid returns to a simmer, add the celery, carrots, onions, bouquet garni, and peppercorns. Simmer for about 2 hours longer, skimming frequently.

Remove from the stove and let the stock stand for at least 30 minutes.

Set a fine strainer over a large container and ladle the stock into the strainer. Discard the liquid at the very bottom of the pot, since this is likely to contain impurities.

To cool the stock quickly, set the container in ice (fill up your sink with ice water to do this).

Refrigerate for up to 48 hours, or transfer to smaller containers and freeze.

VEAL STOCK

✽ *Makes 10 quarts*

THIS RECIPE will require a very large stockpot; if you do not have one, the amounts can easily be halved.

8 pounds veal knuckles	1½ cups celery, cut into 1-inch lengths
2 calf's feet, split	2 cups white mushrooms
2 pounds chicken wings	5 cloves garlic, skin left on
2 pounds veal shoulder, cut into chunks	1 bouquet garni—about 15 Italian parsley stems, 20 sprigs thyme, and 3 bay leaves
10 quarts cold water	
4 quarts ice cubes	2 tablespoons crushed white peppercorns
½ cup sunflower oil	
2 cups carrots, cut into 1-inch lengths	1 cup tomato paste
2 cups onions, cut into chunks	
1 cup leeks, cut into 1-inch lengths	

In a very large stockpot, combine all the meats. Add the cold water and ice. Bring to a simmer over medium heat.

Meanwhile, place a large sauté pan over high heat. Add 2 tablespoons of the oil and sauté the carrots for about 5 minutes, until slightly colored. Transfer to a colander to drain the excess fat. Repeat for the onions, leeks, and celery, adding 2 tablespoons oil for each batch. Drain the fat from all the sautéed vegetables and spread on a large tray.

As soon as the stock starts to simmer, begin skimming the surface carefully to remove any impurities. Once impurities have mostly stopped rising, add the sautéed vegetables, mushrooms, garlic, bouquet garni, and white peppercorns. When the stock returns to the simmer, skim again. Add the tomato paste and simmer for at least 12 hours, or up to 16 hours, skimming the surface frequently. When the stock is finished, remove from the heat and let stand for at least 1 hour.

Continued

Set a fine strainer over a large container and ladle the stock into the strainer. Discard the liquid at the very bottom of the pot, since this is likely to contain impurities. The stock can be used as is, or it can be reduced to a demi-glaze.

Chill the container of stock in ice water in the sink, then refrigerate or freeze, or reduce it first as described below.

Pour the strained stock into a pot, bring to a simmer over medium-low heat, and simmer until it is reduced to 6 cups; it will have a syrupy, sauce-like consistency.

Transfer to a container and chill in an ice bath, then refrigerate for up to 48 hours or transfer to smaller containers and freeze. You can freeze this reduced stock in ice cube trays, then pop the cubes out and store in the freezer in heavy plastic bags to add to a sauce or other dish.

FISH STOCK

❀ *Makes 8 cups*

THE BEST BONES for fish stock are from sole or turbot. Halibut and flounder are good, too. Avoid oily fish, such as salmon or bluefish.

4 pounds bones from white-fleshed fish

2 tablespoons canola oil

6 shallots, sliced

1 small fennel bulb, thinly sliced

1 cup diced (½-inch) celery

2 garlic cloves, skin left on

2 cups dry white wine, such as Verdicchio or Pinot Grigio

3 cups cold water

4 cups ice cubes

1 bouquet garni—5 Italian parsley stems, 3 sprigs tarragon, 3 sprigs thyme

1 teaspoon crushed white peppercorns

Rinse the fish bones thoroughly, making sure that they are free of gills and blood. (I then leave the bones in a bucket under slowly running water for about 2 hours, stirring from time to time.) Drain well. Chop the bones, roughly, into 2-inch pieces.

Heat the oil in a large stockpot over medium-low heat. Add the shallots, fennel, celery, and garlic and sauté for 7 to 8 minutes, or until soft and translucent. Add the fish bones and increase the heat to medium. Add the white wine and bring to a simmer, stirring with a wooden spoon or spatula to loosen the browned bits on the bottom of the pot. Simmer until the liquid is reduced by half, about 10 minutes.

Add the cold water and ice cubes and return to a simmer, skimming any impurities. Add the bouquet garni and peppercorns, reduce the heat, and simmer gently for 20 minutes, skimming frequently. Remove from the heat and let the stock stand for 30 minutes.

Continued

Set a fine strainer over a large container and ladle the stock into the strainer. Discard the liquid at the very bottom of the pot, since it is likely to contain impurities.

Chill the stock in ice water in the sink, then refrigerate for 48 hours or freeze for no more than 1 week.

LE MARCHE WINE

If I had asked you about Le Marche wine ten or fifteen years ago, the chances are that if you knew of any, it was a mass-produced Verdicchio that comes in a green bottle shaped like a fish. Our reputation in the wine world then was one of frivolity. ❋ But there is much more to Le Marche wine than that. Serious wine lovers have been late to discover the virtues of our traditional wines, which have been a bit of a secret even to other Italians. As with our gastronomy, this is due in part to the isolation of Le Marche. But there is also the factor that Marchigiani are reputed to drink more wine than the other citizens of Italy; perhaps we have not exported much wine because there was so little left over. In any case, our wines have not, until very recently, competed in the global market, nor have they aspired to the sophistication of the Super Tuscans and the Barolos.

But change has come to Le Marche, and our distance from the wine scene may have been to our benefit; much of the trendy overoaking and overaging of wines that has afflicted other winemakers whose ambitions exceeded the quality of the grapes has largely been avoided. Marchigiani are, by history, tradition, and character, well suited to small production—and now to the care and attention required to take the wines of antiquity to a high level of refinement and drinkability.

Our most famous grape, Verdicchio, has been cultivated at least since Greek times. It may, in fact be a descendent of a Greek Trebbiano. There are two traditional DOCs (the Italian version of the French AOC) for Verdicchio. Just west of Ancona, very near to my hometown of Osimo, we have the Verdicchio di Castelli di Jesi. Fruity, spirited, and lean, the wine carries notes of peach, apple, even kiwi. It is ready to drink, in fact often best to drink, after only a year of aging. Sergio Esposito, of Italian Wine Merchants in New York City, spends more time in Le Marche than any importer I know, and he is a tremendous aficionado of the Verdicchios made by Sartarelli. He has described them as "having great minerality that is lively on the palate, explosive and fresh . . . well balanced, with beautiful bursts of fruits that are fresh and tangy." More and more, our Verdicchios are tending to this elegance, and everyone who has tried a great one agrees there is no better wine to complement fish.

Further inland, Verdicchio di Matelica is produced at higher altitudes. Traditionally the vines produce grapes of greatly concentrated flavor, resulting in wines of great depth. Typically they benefit from aging. In fact they must be aged for at least twenty-four months. These are among the driest of the Verdicchios, well balanced and fruity but not overripe.

If Verdicchios are the wine for fish, Le Marche reds are the wines with the structure, body, and power to stand up to the big flavors of robust meat dishes like porchetta. The major red wines of Le Marche are Rosso Conero and Rosso Piceno. Rosso Conero is produced in the region of Mt. Conero, the last upthrust of the Apennines, where wine-makers such as Moroder use predominantly Montepulciano and Sangiovese grapes to produce powerful wines of complexity and charm. One of the most highly regarded modern producers, Antonio Terni of Fattoria le Terrazze, left out the Sangiovese in his widely acclaimed full-bodied Conero that is 100 percent Montepulciano. It has ripe sweet tannins that provide structure for the rich black cherry tones of the wine. He attracted somewhat bemused admiration to this wine when, in tribute to his musical idol, Bob Dylan, he created "Visions of J" (Visions of Johanna). Another of his wines, Chaos, a blend of Montepulciano, Merlot, and Syrah, sought after by wine lovers, might be called a "Super Marchigiano."

There are two types of Rosso Piceno, which comes from the largest DOC in Le Marche, in the southern part of the region. The regular "garden variety" Rosso Piceno is a fruity and flowery wine with good tannins. It's very drinkable after a year but can be quite nice, even improved, after three or four years. Rosso Piceno Superiore comes only from vineyards on the south-facing bank of the Tronto River. Often higher in the percentage of Montepulciano than regular Rosso Piceno, it develops deeper and fuller structure with age. One of our favorites at Maestro, especially with boar and squab, is Rosso Piceno Superiore Vigna Monte Prandone, 2001. It is powerful and full of the flavor of dark berries.

SOURCES

ARTISANAL CHEESE CENTER
Tel. 877-797-1200
www.artisanalcheese.com

❈ *Italian and other fine cheeses*

BROWNE TRADING COMPANY
Tel. 800-944-7848
www.browne-trading.com

❈ *crayfish, langoustines, diver scallops, prawns, cuttlefish, bone-in salt cod, turbot,
orata, and other European fish (some of these may need to be special-ordered)*

D'ARTAGNAN
Tel. 800-327-8246
www.dartagnan.com

❈ *wild mushrooms (fresh and dried) and truffles; chestnuts; jumbo quail; wild boar*

EURO GOURMET
Tel. 301-937-2888

❊ *extra-large rigatoni, Campofilone pasta, and high-quality olive oil, including Gabrielloni from Le Marche*

ITALIAN FOODS CORPORATION
Tel. 510-444-9050
www.italianfoods.com

❊ *Campofilone pasta*

LATIN MERCHANTS
Tel. 206-223-9374
www.latinmerchant.com

❊ *manteca (soft lard)*

MANICARETTI
www.manicaretti.com

❊ *Italian ingredients and products of all types, including Corbezzolo honey and polenta flour; Manicaretti is an importer, but its website lists retail outlets and on-line sources that carry its products, including Market Hall Foods (www.markethallfoods.com; tel. 888-952-4005 for mail-order)*

NIMAN RANCH
Tel. 866-808-0340
www.nimanranch.com

❊ *guanciale, organic pork chops and other meats*

RITROVO ITALIAN REGIONAL FOODS
Tel. 206-985-1635
www.ritrovo.com

❊ *Tenuta di Castello farro and Carnaroli rice*

SALUMERIA BIELLESE
Tel. 212-736-7376
www.salumeriabiellese.com

❀ *cotechino and other salume/charcuterie*

SUR LA TABLE
Tel. 800-243-0852
www.surlatable.com

❀ *panettone molds and other kitchenware*

TODARO BROTHERS
Tel. 877-472-2767
www.todarobros.com

❀ *Italian 00 flour and other Italian ingredients*

TRUE FOODS MARKET
Tel. 800-758-8245
www.truefoodsmarket.com

❀ *almond flour*

ZINGERMAN'S
Tel. 888-636-8162
www.zingermans.com

❀ *Corbezzolo honey, polenta, olives (including Taggiasche), and other specialty ingredients*

INDEX

ℬ

Grapes, in Roasted Veal Chops with
    Honey, 146–47
Greens, Ravioli with Fresh Herbs and, in
    Lemon Butter, 60–62
Grigliata Mista di Pesci, 96–98
Grilled:
  Beef Tenderloin with Fondue of
    Talamello Cheese, 148
  Country Bread, Crayfish Soup with,
    47–48
  Dover Sole, 101–2
  Eggplant Graziella-Style, 22–23
  Mixed Grill of Fish and Shellfish, 96–98
  Monkfish with Artichokes, Garlic, and
    Sage, 113–14
  Orata with Anchovy Sauce, 109–10
  Pork Chops, My Father's, 157–58
  Pork Liver with Bay Leaf, 164–65
  Spit-Roasted Squab, 139–40
  Trout with Black Truffles and Anchovy
    Pesto, 115–16
Grilling over charcoal, regulating heat in,
  22
Grottamare, 9, 81
Guanciale:
  Bucatini with, 70–71
  source for, 224
Guinea Hen, Braised, 137–38

H

Hamilton, Lady Emma, 191
Harvest feasts:
  for grape harvest, 200
  for wheat harvest and threshing, 134
Hay, Smoky, Turbot in, 117–18
Honey:
  corbezzolo, 146
  Corbezzolo, sources for, 224, 225

Roasted Veal Chops with, 146–47
Vanilla Custard, 180–81
Walnut Bread, 201–2

I

Italian Foods Corporation, 224
Italian Talisman Cookbook (Boni), 188
Italian Wine Merchants, New York City,
  220

J

John Dory, in Fish Stew, 121–23

K

Kitchenware, source for, 225

L

Lamb:
  Easter, 171–73
  Fritto Misto of Zucchini, Artichokes
    and, 168–70
Langoustines:
  Campofilone Pasta with, 65–66
  with Fried Cauliflower and Tomato
    Sauce, 90–91
Lard, soft (manteca, or *manteca de
    puerco*), 24
  source for, 224
Lasagne, Le Marche, 8, 75–78
Latin Merchants, 224
Lattarolo, 180–81
Leopardi, Giacomo, 8–9

Rosso Conero, 221

Rosso Piceno, 221

S

T